Animating Guarini

Savannah,

Congratulations on your
thesis! I wish you
the best.

May, 2021

Published by Applied Research and Design Publishing,
an imprint of ORO Editions.
Gordon Goff: Publisher

www.appliedresearchanddesign.com
info@appliedresearchanddesign.com

With contributions by Perry Kulper
Book Design by Jessica Greenfield
Copy Editor: Cameron Macdonell
Project Manager: Jake Anderson

10 9 8 7 6 5 4 3 2 1 First Edition

ISBN: 978-1-943532-74-2

Color Separations and Printing: ORO Group Ltd.
Printed in China.

AR+D Publishing makes a continuous effort to minimize the overall carbon
footprint of its publications. As part of this goal, AR+D, in association with
Global ReLeaf, arranges to plant trees to replace those used in the manufacturing of the paper produced for its books. Global ReLeaf is an international
campaign run by American Forests, one of the world's oldest nonprofit
conservation organizations. Global ReLeaf is American Forests' education
and action program that helps individuals, organizations, agencies, and
corporations improve the local and global environment by planting and caring
for trees.

Animating Guarini

AN ORTHOGRAPHIC PROJECT

By Mark Ericson

With a Foreword by Perry Kulper

For Camille and Monroe

Contents

Foreword by Perry Kulper   *ix*

Ordinary Geometry   1

PART 1

On Redrawing   7

Reassembling Guarini   19

Guarini Reassembled   35

PART 2

Animating Guarini   55

Guarini Animated   71

APPENDIX

Guarini Explained   131

Acknowledgments   *179*

Image Credits   *181*

Foreword

PERRY KULPER

Teased Eyes and a Triggered Imagination

I remember the first time I laid eyes on them. They were blue, a kind of bluish gray: tantalizingly beautiful. All kinds of catalysts fired—relational contours were awakened, jostled about, and reassembled. Their myriad associations transported me to other worlds—worlds implicated in Mark Ericson's drawings. My mind raced and hasn't slowed since. I thought about Yves Klein and "that" blue. I also remembered slightly faded blueprints from days gone past, and Krzysztof Kieslowski's enigmatic film *Three Colors: Blue* locked in—blue lighting, blue objects, and the sky. I couldn't help but think about a series of bluish-gray things, a new geometric species, mandala-like in their nature—collections, a taxonomy of a new sort, incredible assemblies of insects carefully attached and tagged, and birds just as carefully staged and registered, brought into a different light. These, and many, many more associations drifted across my memory and imagination. And new questions arose. Were these new, vaguely recognizable, though indeterminate specimens that might be collected, reflected upon, and critically positioned and poised to construct new forms of knowledge—while augmenting representational ethics and practices? Emphatically, yes. And what else might lie under the surface, behind the scenes, under the metaphorical car hood of Mark's bluish grays?

Opposite
Onto an Epicycle of Cones of Four
Sides, Elevation Oblique, Version 09

Dialed In

In more disciplinarily specific terms, and upon further reflection, other things emerged. These bluish-gray, geometric, quasi-atmospheric constructions seem to belong to the history of ideas and to families of representational types, such as anamorphosis, accelerated and decelerated perspective, and cubism—visualizations that made sense of their references while opening an entirely different range of conversations about spatial developments as related to a real politics of communication. By prying it open, testing its genetic makeup and latent potential, Mark has reimagined orthography as a fertile, rerouted drawing technique— revealed in front of, behind, and up the sleeve of its default assumptions.

I was also thinking of the contemporary and critically important German visual artist Gerhard Richter and his deliberate and disciplined work in both photography and painting. His lifelong pursuits have accomplished several things, not the least of which is his insightful ruminations on the history of painting. It's instructive to see Mark's work in this light, where the history of architectural drawing establishes Mark's disciplined efforts, and his work with the rudiments of our discipline for extended periods of time. This endeavor is especially relevant, even poignant, in an age when avant-garde influences still run deep, preferring instantaneous presence, disruption, and continuous rupture as cultural horizons.

I couldn't help but think about atmospheric geometries, or what I imagine to be such. My conceptual imagination launched to other places otherwise uninhabited. I'm not entirely sure what I mean by this, but I am provoked by thinking about geometry and its roles from an entirely different perspective, inspired by Mark's extraordinary work—atmospheric geometries and the worlds implicated therein. Phew! In parallel, drawn mandalas and labyrinthine puzzles crept into my imagination—animating a kind of metaphorical wilderness in bluish gray, mesmeric in its beauty and enigmatic in its purpose. The drawings have real presence, and I knew something was at stake, in deep play. For keeps.

Upon reflection, and theoretically considered, Mark's efforts are partially rooted in the work, writings, and teaching of the late British architect, teacher, and historian Robin Evans—particularly the latter's reflections on stereotomy in the posthumous publication, *The Projective Cast*. Paris based theorist, industrial designer, and architect Bernard Cache's influences lie nearby—specifically his work on the image as nonrepresentational and constructive. Mark's project is also broadly situated in relation to Martin Kemp's elucidations on issues of visualization, modeling, and representation in *The Science of Art*. More recently, I observed possible connections in Mark's work to Preston Scott Cohen's interest in geometric conundrums, specifically demonstrated in Cohen's work on the Sacristy of San Carlo ai Catinari in Rome; to Pablo Garcia's interests in digitality, through relations of the virtual and the real; and on to Miles Ritter's commitments to descriptive geometry and the technologies of representation. All these characters are important in the continuities of the discourse linked to the roles, capacities, practices, and ethics of representation—and toward drawings and their varied cultural agencies: spatial and representational. Mark participates in, synthesizes, and is generating new disciplinary knowledge in carefully orchestrated works and insights surrounding the mechanics of orthographic projection—in relation to ongoing discursive and practiced developments in drawing, architecture, and the construction of visual culture more broadly.

Chromosomal Seeding

To digress...Mark lives parallel lives. He's contemporary, but his heart is often tracking elsewhere— traversing other topographies, in another era, another generation, another set of conversations on, underneath, and through the deeply structured plane of representation. His work is likewise contemporary, but it, too, lies elsewhere—he's a time traveler, an another-epoch wannabe.

His project is patient, provocative, and pithy, not to mention painstakingly precise. Period. Okay, enough with the p's, except one more that fits: probative. Fundamentally, Mark's dogged pursuits challenge assumptions we make about architectural drawing and about the capacities, let's say the potential, of precedents, both spatial and representational. Questions surrounding measure, calibration, and analysis, unpacking things from a generative perspective—as they were in his days as a graduate student at the Southern California Institute of Architecture (SCI-Arc) in Los Angeles—remain central to his work.

In 2005, Mark participated in "Eccentric Form + Material Ecstasy," a vertical studio offered at SCI-Arc where we asked questions about contemporary prospects of the surrealist project—the culture-changing work that flourished in the early part of the twentieth century. We wondered if there might be any merit in rethinking, reframing, and redeploying surrealist tactics (e.g., juxtaposition of distant realities, familiar strangeness, extraordinary ordinariness, paradoxical illusion, and structuring the shockingly unexpected) or in rebooting surrealist values, spatially, for contemporary society. We were committed to reconsidering surrealist approaches, on the hunt for potential spatial, psychological, and experiential connections where there had been none—all in a contemporary context.

The studio also offered the possibility that processes to produce the work, including the work of an architectural drawing, might be active—that its generative roles might be worthwhile, considering architectural drawing as more than just a benign accomplice, default tool, or instrument of visualization. We thus advocated for the generative potential of the architectural drawing, strategically framed and deployed, perhaps bringing so-called content and increased ideational density to the table of our work. Additionally, we were careful to critically frame key surrealist precedents, offering ways in which the use of precedents might be active and not simply acknowledged as innocent bystanders. In addition to the specific content of the studio, Mark probed Salvador Dali's painting *Angelus of Gala*, poking at the relations between an observer and the observed—a bit akin to Michel Foucault's observations of the infamous *Las Meninas*, painted by the revered Spanish painter Diego Velasquez, in *The Order of Things*. From a designer's perspective, he activated a passive ground by producing maps, aerial imaging, and parallel information, translated through a strategy of framing and measurement in California's Owens Valley. By implicating analogous relations of drawing constructions, and the site to discover areas neglected by the conventions of architectural representation, the processes of measuring, and of copying and repeating, became an underlying infrastructure, a kind of mantra for Mark's work.

Subsequent to the studio work, Mark's thesis, "Cartographies of Discrepancy," interrogated differences, arguably discrepancies, between techniques of mapping and physical grounds or specific situations. One particular situation was mapped as a critical instrument—as a generative tool for structuring relations between architecture and an assumed site. Through the production of quasi-neurosurgical drawings, alongside physical constructs, Mark structured relations between a spatial proposal and a politically, and operationally, disputed site, Okinotori—a subtly visible disruption in the surface of the Pacific Ocean near Japan. His interests were sparked by a dispute between China and Japan about whether this amphibious condition qualified as land and under whose authority it existed. His thesis proposition used differing points of view about this surface quality, and their discrepancies, to structure five independent grounds—these cartographically specific topographies based on the various dispositions, and their implicated values, toward the definition of Okinotori. The grounds were understood as cartographic ciphers, kinds of intelligent inscriptions that represented the discrepant points of view. Here, the site was not understood as a specifically defined surface break, as a topography in a conventional sense, but rather as a process of definition and construction.

In both bodies of work, the studio and thesis, Mark developed a specific and precise discipline for working, tailored to the interests of the work. He discovered and invented techniques of inquiry, concocted programmatic logics, and mined representational potential toward a loaded and provocative spatial, and representational, proposition. Importantly, the practices and ethical bearing of representational techniques were used to reveal the politics of interpretation hinged to varied points of view about Okinotori.

I believe both works that Mark accomplished in his final year at SCI-Arc are still resonant in his teaching and design research—the genetic or chromosomal structure formulated some years ago. This earlier academic work demonstrates his real curiosity, his hunger in fact, for discovering what might be discussed and discovered through methods of working and representational techniques—feeding his insatiable appetite for scrutinizing representational conventions for lost, found, and phantom lives. By working through partial sets of information, by inventing geometric translations, and by recognizing and then capitalizing on the latent capacities of architectural drawing, he is rerouting the ageless legacies of architectural representation—locating them in the history of disciplinary knowledge while facilitating new potential for their agencies.

A View with a Dash of Distance

Like many invested in critical pedagogy, in spatial and cultural advances, in the agencies of architecture, and in the generative capacities of representation, I have followed Mark's work, research initiatives, and teaching achievements with more than great interest. The quality of his questions, the nature of his inquiries, the quantity of his knowledge about age-old drawing and representational conventions interfacing with emergent technologies—alongside invented techniques—is extraordinary, groundbreaking in fact. Equally, his talent to craft precisely drawn constructions, his ability to contextualize his work in the larger history of representation, and his situationally specific approaches to representational techniques all

recommend serious consideration of his increasingly rich probes. Undeniably, he is a role model for many committed to the construction of the discipline of architecture and to integrated thinking as related to its allied practices, disciplines, and education.

While I know him to be an accomplished and influential teacher, Mark's primary contributions lie in his creative practice and research. Neither in the realm of artistic production, nor in that of purely scholarly research, he occupies a still emerging and fertile ground or platform for creative production: design research. This is an oft-overused term, but in this case, his work is helping to shape those conversations, as architects extend the boundaries of the definition of the architect and what constitutes practice. By theorizing various material and representational practices and materializing various theoretical approaches, especially through interpretive drawings, his work participates in multiple disciplinary strains and cultural practices. These include developments in geometry, mathematics, optics, mapping, projective representational systems, and digital technologies. He occupies a rare position that values the deep consequences of the history of representation, without abandoning or succumbing to historical recall. Rather, he is interested in painstakingly autopsying and unraveling historically grounded types of representation, specifically by constructively referring to the work of the great Italian priest, writer, mathematician, and architect of the Baroque period: Guarino Guarini. He is dogged in chasing possible conversations and outcomes that the disassembly and reconstruction of orthography might have with contemporary patterns of thought—most specifically with emerging digital practices. He doesn't privilege one over the other. Rather, he looks for productive and synthetic interfaces of both toward the formation of new disciplinary knowledge and innovative representational strategies and techniques. His generative use of history and theory is a model from which we can all benefit.

The Next Roads

Mark's visual elucidations on Guarini are possessive, instructional, and exceptional to say the least. The work trades on the history of ideas and developments in optics and mathematics, not to mention relations between drawing conventions, techniques, and spatial possibilities. Revering history but not imprisoned by it, his work draws out the capacities to translate, even interpret, powerful historical evidence, looking to construct new crimes from existing evidence while rerouting the roles and techniques of orthographic projection. The work gets under the metaphorical car hood of orthography, tickling a whole range of subject areas inherently hitched to its legacy, and transformation.

The cultural background structure and the roles of orthography have changed since Guarini's time. But, perhaps the deeper structural principles of the capacities of representation (orthography in particular) remain constant. At the same time, it may be that Mark is in the business of discovering (inventing, as it were) latent lives to which the techniques and deeper histories respond, albeit from altered points of view. This is one of the real insights and contributions of his labors of love—that is, using orthographic techniques, rendered through Guarini's analogic lens, while developing a critical mode of inquiry, opening new investigations to make new sense of representational systems, far too often taken for granted.

Returning to interests in discrepancies between seemingly similar things, this work exceeds translation, historical recall, or simply rebooting orthographic projection. Rather, Mark looks to analysis (with more than just formal questions at stake) to develop a discipline for working, for design researching, for developing a mode of critical inquiry, while projecting what might be possible. Mark considers the labor of architectural drawing and its explicit and implicit content, rather than simply imitating historical precedents, copying Guarini, or representing spatial conditions. And while his work is specific and precise, it seems to me that he has set up a critical mode of inquiry that might not simply be beholden to the subjects of his curiosity; it might also allow us to bask in the pleasure of his extraordinary accomplishments and contributions while seeing the work as establishing a discipline for working on work, no matter the subjects of one's attention. This is a true gift to a discipline wrestling with its own definition and the definition(s) of the architect, not to mention the increasingly enlarged roles of spatial representation—to which Mark's work contributes a whole bunch of key chromosomes.

It is a true pleasure to realize how much quality work, focused through a particular set of lenses, Mark has accomplished. I look forward to his next gravities—to his next penetrating, probative, and puzzling forays into the transformative wilderness of spatial representation. Bridging precedents, positioned values, theoretical and practical insights, and structural contributions, this work is the real deal, and this guy is pure talent. I won't lose track of him soon, and I would recommend that you don't either.

—Perry Kulper

Ordinary Geometry

Notice that I have been able to describe the fantastic worlds above imagined without ceasing to employ the language of ordinary geometry.

— Henri Poincare, Science and Hypothesis, 1913

In architecture, there is no more ordinary drawing than an orthographic projection. As a geometric operation that generates three-dimensional forms from two-dimensional drawings, it has existed at least since the sixteenth century.[1] Over its nearly five hundred–year history, orthographic projection evolved from a geometric technique for the generation of form to the modern convention of orthographic drawing—a codified standard for the visual representation of buildings in plan, section, and elevation. This shift from a geometric technique to a representational convention, divested architecture of its geometric foundations.[2]

Recent shifts in the discipline have increased the distance between the technique of orthographic projection and the convention of orthographic drawing. Beginning with architects who adopted personal computers in the 1990s, tools such as animation and digital modeling displaced orthographic projection as the primary abstract generator of architectural form.[3] Despite these changes in the design process, the orthographic drawings of plan, section, and elevation have continued as the conventions of architectural representation. The move from geometric technique to representational convention has thus removed orthographic projection almost entirely from the

Opposite
Onto an Epicycle of Tori, Oblique
Projection, Oriented, Version 07

discipline, even while the convention of orthographic drawing persists. In this book, I consider an alternative, examining the generative drawing methods of orthographic projection that have been lost or discarded in the evolution from technique to convention. I argue that these techniques and not their resolution in plan, section, and elevation have continued relevance in the development of architectural drawing.

Orthographic drawing is a convention of representation used to describe the shape of a building in both built and unbuilt works of architecture. It works by projecting the form of a building onto an imagined perpendicular plane with parallel lines. This plane, often referred to as the picture plane, is isomorphic with the drawing surface. In an elevation drawing, for example, the picture plane is perpendicular to the ground and parallel to a surface of the building, providing the proportionally accurate size and shape of everything on the outside of the building that is parallel to the plane. This is where the orthographic drawing gains its utility—by providing accurate dimensional information in the form of flattened views. When we look at an orthographic drawing, we are looking at an abstracted view of a building in which all three-dimensional information has been flattened onto a plane so that it can both be seen and measured. This is different than a perspective projection, which uses converging lines for the projection onto the picture plane, creating the illusion of depth.

Historically, orthographic projections were constructed on paper or stone as a drawing operation to project information between plans, elevations and sections with the aid of parallel lines. This technique, sometimes labeled combined orthographic projection, was probably first presented in print by Albrecht Dürer in the fifteenth century.[4] Within contemporary architecture, the use of digital tools has obviated the need for this drawing process. A building form is developed three-dimensionally in a digital model, and then a secondary function is to extract the plans, sections, and elevations from the model.[5]

The encapsulation of the process of orthographic drawing into a secondary function further cements its status as a convention. By removing almost all direct engagement with the geometric techniques that underlie the process, orthographic projection has been simplified to a single and predictable outcome, an abstracted view of a building—an orthographic drawing. However, in the development of the technique of orthographic projection, a variety of drawings were created that did not deal with the production of plans, sections, and elevations. In some extreme cases, the drawings were used as graphic calculators, providing distance without form. These drawings, tied to the production of stonecutting templates, present a divergent history of architectural drawing—a history of architectural drawing in which the generation of form was independent of the conventions of visual representation, a history of drawing form without seeing it.

Orthographic projection is now a precise term to denote a specific geometric operation. However, its history as a term has been inclusive of other forms of drawing no longer practiced. Stereotomy, one such form, is a long-defunct drawing practice that enabled masons to accurately define the shape of the individual stones assembled to produce vaults and domes. The term was probably first used in print by stonemason Jacques Curabelle in 1644 in an attempt to legally bind the practice to stonemasonry, but it had a much earlier point of origin.[6] It emerged in Paleochristian Syria and was likely brought back to Europe after the Crusades.[7] Both before and after Curabelle's use of the term, stereotomy was referred to by multiple names, including the art of lines and orthographic projection.[8] Thus, while orthographic projection is often understood as a specific type of architectural drawing, it history binds it to the practice of stereotomy through a set of shared names.

As a drawing technique for the generation and measurement of three-dimensional forms on a two-dimensional surface, stereotomy precedes Gaspard Monge's codification of descriptive geometry in 1795. Unlike descriptive geometry, the practice of stereotomy does not rely entirely upon the apparatus of imagined planes to understand and represent views of an object. Instead, it is dependent on the redeployment of Euclid's geometric principles.[9] Its primary focus is on the measurement, by any means possible, of the individual lines that direct and generate surfaces. Proportion, logical argument, and projection are intermingled to solve problems in the description and generation of form. In fact, scholars continue to debate whether stereotomy is a discipline of drawing or a discipline of construction and statics.[10] While the objective of this process is to produce form and space from a heavy volumetric material, its instrumental practices depended greatly on the abstract manipulation of lines and the physical manipulation of light paper models.[11] Thus, despite its link to the production of stone buildings, stereotomy's techniques and processes are positioned firmly as a drawing practice.

Unlike modern orthographic drawings, the focus of stereotomy is to produce accurate measurements with as little drawing as possible. If a three-dimensional object could be generated and measured with only two lines, it was, without resorting to visual representation. A typical example of this is the drawing of a cone in the development of a toroidal vault as a right triangle, describing only the rotational profile of the figure (FIGURE 1.1). The vertical line beginning at point *K* at the center of the drawing is the axis of every cone in drawing. Each individual cone is drawn as a diagonal line intersecting this vertical axis, such as the line that intersects the vertical axis at point 6. The perpendicular distance from the vertical line and the end of any diagonal line provides the radius of the cone. The height difference between the two endpoints of any diagonal line provides the height of the cone. Yet there is no drawing of a view of the cone as it might appear to the eye. Instead, it has been described by its geometric properties: height, radius, and axis. Stereotomic drawings were made to both generate and measure form, without dependency on visual representation. While the conventions of orthographic drawing have reduced this technique to a single task and bound it to representation, its actual evolution from stereotomy is not so reductive.

At the end of the nineteenth century, with the rise of concrete and iron building technologies, complex two-dimensional drawings for stonecutting began to lose their practical relevance.[12] Orthographic drawing continued to be the dominant mode of architectural representation, and even a cursory survey of current technologies shows its consistent presence. However, instead of perpetuating the assumption that orthographic drawing and stereotomy are two distinct forms of drawing, it is more useful to understand them as the same and to see the demise of stereotomy not as the end of an obscure drawing methodology but rather the loss of the geometric techniques foundational

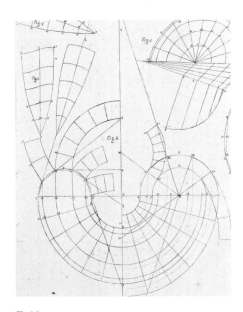

Fig 1.1
Guarino Guarini, *Architettura civile*, Trattato IV, Lastra XIV
The drawing for the stereotomic development of a toroidal vault.

for orthographic projection. What remains is a simplified technique, lacking the ability to describe and generate complex forms because it has been reduced to a single task: visual representation.[13]

Animating Guarini begins with this dilemma. In this book, I analyze the geometric and instrumental history of orthographic projection to propose an alternate understanding of both the origins and potential futures of that technique. Fundamental to this book are the drawings of Italian architect Guarino Guarini (1624–83). Guarini was the architect of significant religious buildings, such as San Lorenzo (1687) and Santissima Sindone (1694) in Turin, Italy. His treatise on architecture, *Architettura civile* (1737), was published long after his death in 1683, completed by another architect, Bernardo Vittone, from an unfinished manuscript.[14] The fourth tractate of the treatise, "Dell'ortografia gettata," focuses on the use of orthographic projection to generate and accurately describe vaults and domes.[15] It is often cited as an instance of orthographic projection used to generate more complex forms from simple ones, and by projecting semicircles onto various surfaces, Guarini derived an array of nameless curves.[16] His techniques ranged from the standard production of views to the definition of objects as a set of graphic proportions without shape. Orthographic projection, for Guarini, was thus an open framework used to solve the metric description of objects in the most expedient manner possible. Guarini's drawings present orthographic projection as a malleable set of geometric techniques centered on the generation and measurement of form in lieu of adherence to the conventions of representation.

Animating Guarini is divided into three sections. The first centers on the analysis of Guarini's drawings and text. In it, I reconstruct Guarini's techniques from fragments of drawings, text, and references, generating single orthographic projections from which a set of observations are derived. These new drawings use the computer as no more than an enhanced drawing device, adhering to the logic of drafting but transposing it into a computer. At the core of this work is a formal analysis of Guarini's methods—proposing a new future for historical objects. In the book's second section, I focus on the transformation of the first section's formal analysis into animated drawings, thus incorporating time and motion. The animation stills in this section present a set of proposals for orthographic projection, linking seventeenth-century drawing techniques with strategies specific to the computer. And the third section comprises a manual on orthographic projection, providing instructions on how to complete a series of projections derived from Guarini. This section is a small step in opening up some of the arguments posited in this book, exposing them to deeper technical inquiry. It can be used as a means to understand and question the underlying arguments of the text, or it can be used as a starting point for further study of orthographic projection.

Conclusion

The evolution of orthographic projection from a technique to a convention has provided architecture with orthographic drawing—a form of imaging continually used to present, defend, and build architecture. Orthographic projection's geometric principles and complex history are no longer part of an architect's education, and yet its underlying Euclidean geometry informs the materialization of architecture, regardless of complexity.[17] In this book, I mine the instrumental history of orthographic projection to reacquire the generative techniques of drawing that do not deal with visualization. *Animating Guarini* is thus a historical account and a reimagining of orthographic projection as a drawing technique that precedes convention.

1   Wolfgang Lefèvre, "The Emergence of Combined Orthographic Projection," in *Picturing Machines 1400–1700*, ed. Wolfgang Lefèvre (Cambridge, MA: MIT Press, 2004), 209–44, 226.

2   Robin Evans, *The Projective Cast: Architecture and Its Three Geometries* (Cambridge, MA: MIT Press, 1995), 327–28.

3   Mario Carpo, ed., *The Digital Turn in Architecture 1992–2012* (Chichester: Wiley, 2013), 8–14, 9.

4   Lefèvre, "Emergence of Combined Orthographic Projection," 226.

5   John May, "Everything Is Already an Image," *Log*, no. 40 (Spring/Summer 2017): 9–26, 19.

6   Giuseppe Fallacara, "Digital Stereotomy and Topological Transformations: Reasoning about Shape Building," in *Proceedings of the Second International Congress on Construction History*, vol. 1, eds. Malcolm Dunkeld, James Campbell, Hentie Louw. Michael Tutton, Bill Addis, Robert Thorne (Exeter: Short Run Press, 2006) 1075–92, 1076 .

7   Joël Sakarovitch, "Stereotomy, A Multifaceted Technique," in *Proceedings of the First International Congress on Construction History*, ed. Santiago Huerta (Madrid: Instituto Juan de Herrera, Escuela Técnica Superior de Arquitectura, 2003) 69–79, 70.

8   Guarini referred to stereotomy as orthographic projection. See Guarino Guarini, *Architettura civile* (Turin: G. Mairesse, 1737), 191.

9   Because stereotomy emerged from stonemasonry it carried forward the reliance on Euclidian geometry from the stone masons of the Middle Ages. See Michele Sbacchi, "Euclidism and Theory of Architecture," *Network Nexus Journal* 3, no. 2 (September 2001): 25–38.

10 Matthias Rippmann, "Funicular Shell Design: Geometric Approaches to Form Finding and Fabrication of Discrete Funicular Structures" (PhD diss., ETH, 2016), 86.

11 Massimo Scolari, *Oblique Drawing: A History of Anti-Perspective* (Cambridge, MA: MIT Press, 2012) 137–63, 51.

12 Sakarovitch, "Stereotomy, A Multifaceted Technique." 74.

13 This loss is mirrored in the continued decrease in the number of architectural programs that offer a course in stereotomy's closest descendent: descriptive geometry—a decline that is best evidenced in architect Mark Burry's description of the near absence of descriptive geometry in his own "late modern" education and the dilemma he faced when confronted with Antoni Gaudí's Sagrada Família. See Mark Burry, "Architecture and Practical Design Computation," in *Computational Design Thinking*, ed. Achim Menges and Sean Ahlquist (London: Wiley, 2011), 102–19.

14 Werner Müller, "The Authenticity of Guarini's Stereotomy in His *Architettura Civile*," *Journal of the Society of Architectural Historians* 27, no. 3 (October 1968): 202–8, 206.

15 Harold A. Meek, *Guarino Guarini and His Architecture* (New Haven, CT: Yale University Press, 1989).

16 Jacqueline Gargus, "Guarino Guarini: Geometrical Transformation and the Invention of New Architectural Meaning," *Harvard Architectural Review* 7 (1989): 116–31, 119.

17 Bernard Cache, "A Plea for Euclid," in *Architecture Words 6: Projectiles*, trans. Clare Barrett and Pamela Johnston (London: AA Publications, 2011), 40.

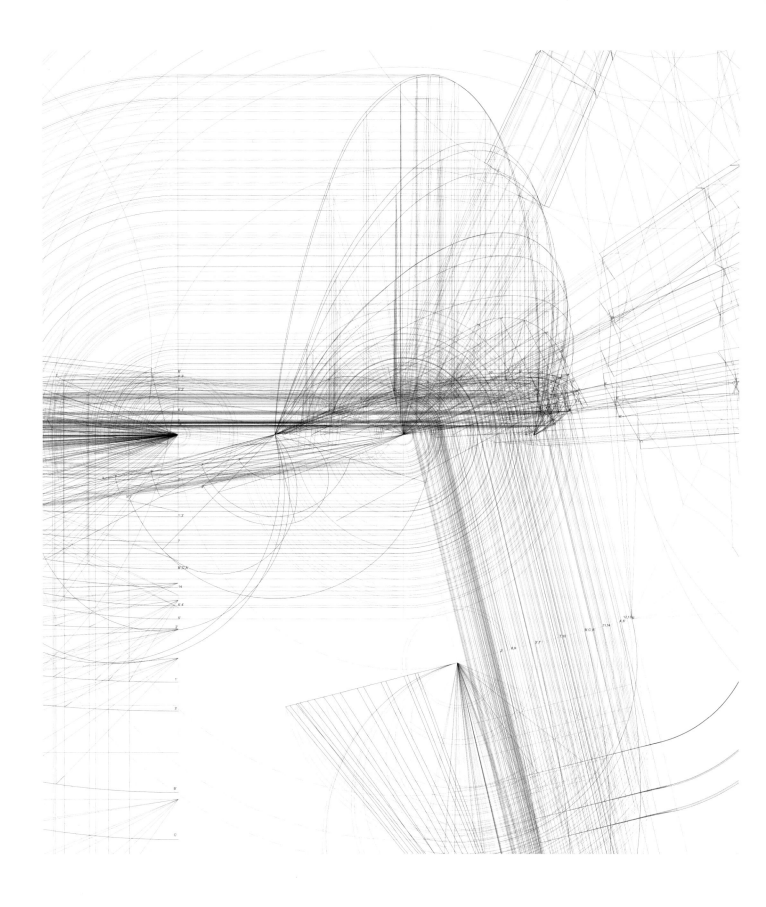

On Redrawing

Because orthographic projection has been central to architecture since the sixteenth century, this centrality makes it is easy to assume that an orthographic projection from the sixteenth century is legible to someone familiar with modern orthographic projection. A plan is a plan. An elevation is an elevation. Little has changed. The recognizable nature of these drawing conventions allows for the appearance of disciplinary continuity and coherence. However, anyone who has ever read a text originally written five hundred years ago is aware of the stylistic, semantic, and syntactical differences among different epochs of the same language. These differences present problems of interpretation and can obscure meaning. Drawings are no different. The style, semantics, and syntax of drawing change over time, making interpretation difficult. Orthographic projection has evolved continuously since its approximate origin in the sixteenth century and was not codified until the end of the eighteenth century.[1] After codification, it became a dead language, carried on as an academic and professional convention. Prior to codification, architects and masons developed idiosyncratic techniques to solve specific formal problems. The possibilities engendered by this open framework allowed for a range of intellectual and creative solutions to similar problems. These techniques were shed over time, leaving a streamlined version of orthographic projection with clear rules and guidelines—a drawing convention. The difference between the modern convention and the uncodified techniques that preceded it demonstrate not only stylistic and syntactical differences but also a very different understanding of drawing—a previous understanding of drawing as comfortable adhering to the conventions of representation as it is with breaking them. Thus, redrawing a centuries-old orthographic projection presents the opportunity to study not only the original drawing but also the differences between it and contemporary practice.

In 1968, art historian Werner Müller published a thorough analysis of a single drawing from Guarini's *Architettura civile*.[2] While other scholars have examined the geometric construction of specific works of Guarini's architecture, Müller was unique in his detailed examination of Guarini's orthographic projections, and his analysis casts doubt on the authenticity of the orthographic projections in *Architettura civile*.[3] He argued that the drawing contains significant errors, errors that Guarini himself would have been unlikely to produce. These errors, Müller continued, demonstrate that the drawings were likely completed by someone else and therefore not authentic examples of Guarini's stereotomy. Furthermore, while Müller used the word "stereotomy" to classify Guarini's drawings, Guarini himself referred to them as orthographic projections.[4] This act of misclassification is telling of Müller's modern understanding of orthographic projection as a representational convention rather than as a formative geometry. Consequently, what Müller assumed to be an error is more likely a fundamental difference in orthographic intent and technique—a difference that positions Guarini's orthographic projection as something distinct from modern codifications.

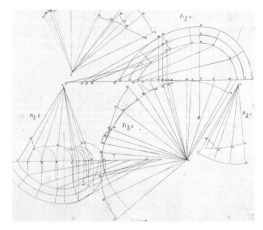

Fig 2.1

An Incomplete Manuscript

Martin Kemp has warned about the risks of redrawing from the perspective of the historian: analysis by drawing lines over images is error-prone and inaccurate to the degree that it compromises the information that the act of redrawing alleges to reveal.[5] Historian Joseph Connors, paraphrasing Rudolf Wittkower, wrote that "the compass in the scholar's hand seldom rebels."[6] This positions the act of faithfully redrawing as a potentially creative act.[7] The historian or architect, may redraw in a manner that best supports their underlying argument. It risks becoming a new drawing with different information, which is also one of the key dilemmas of Guarini's posthumously published *Architettura civile*. Begun by a seventeenth-century architect but completed by another from the eighteenth century, the publication is a redrawing of the original manuscript.

At the beginning of *Architettura civile*, there a section entitled "Avviso a'lettori." This section makes it clear that the book is as much an act of eighteenth-century historical reconstruction as it is the

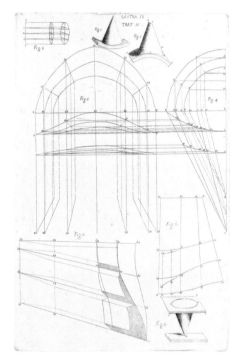

Fig 2.2

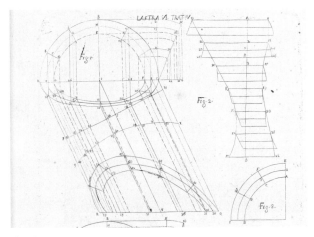

Fig 2.3

Fig 2.1
Guarino Guarini, *Architettura civile*,
Trattato IV, Lastra XI, Figura 4
The drawing of a conic vault cut by a curved surface.

Fig 2.2
Guarino Guarini, *Architettura civile*, Trattato IV, Lastra IX
The drawing of a conoid vault unrolled.

Fig 2.3
Guarino Guarini, *Architettura civile*, Trattato IV, Lastra IV
The drawing of an oblique cylinder cut by an inclined plane.

work of a seventeenth-century architect. The text states that Guarini's death prevented the completion of his work and that the "struggle of cleaning and assembling [it] into one Volume" was Vittone's work.[8] It is impossible to know exactly what "cleaning" and "assembling" entailed, as Guarini's manuscript did not survive.[9] Were all the drawings and text complete, leaving Vittone simply to bind them into the treatise? Did Guarini's manuscript have large gaps that Vittone had to complete himself? In either case, the "Avviso a'lettori" was careful to state that the work was published with "attention, study, and diligence."[10] It is a work of historical analysis and reconstruction, but based on the assumption that the manuscript was incomplete, it is also a new work.

There is evidence in the published text and drawings to support the hypothesis of Guarini's incomplete manuscript. Figure four of plate eleven in the fourth tractate is the drawing of a conic vault cut by a curved surface (FIGURE 2.1). The drawing method is important because it is one of the most general methods that Guarini provided. He stated that it can be used for a cone whose base is elliptical, circular, lenticular, or any other form.[11] What is striking about this drawing is its incompleteness. When considered in relation to some of the other drawings for the fourth tractate, it is missing whole sets of information. Guarini's conoid, from earlier in the tractate, was drawn so that the unrolled stones are displayed flattened on a plane (FIGURE 2.2). The interior surface, exterior surface, and joints were all drawn in their true dimensions. Conversely, Guarini's figure from plate eleven does not unroll the interior surface or the joints, making it an incomplete drawing. Guarini's instructions also end here, stating that the rest can be solved by the "same order," indicating that repeating the previous instructions will solve the remainder of the problem.[12] Its visual difference from most other examples in the fourth tractate suggests that even after Vittone worked on the treatise, some aspects remained incomplete, and that omissions, errors, or brevity might be the product of Guarini's death cutting the work short. If so, Vittone's role was that of assembling the documents of Guarini's manuscript; incomplete drawings were left incomplete. However, Müller argued that Vittone played a much more significant role in its completion.

One Curve, Two Drawings

Müller's analysis centers on the twelfth observation of chapter three in the fourth tractate (FIGURE 2.3). Müller found that both the published text and drawing instruct the reader to perform a geometric error. He compared the erroneous drawing from the

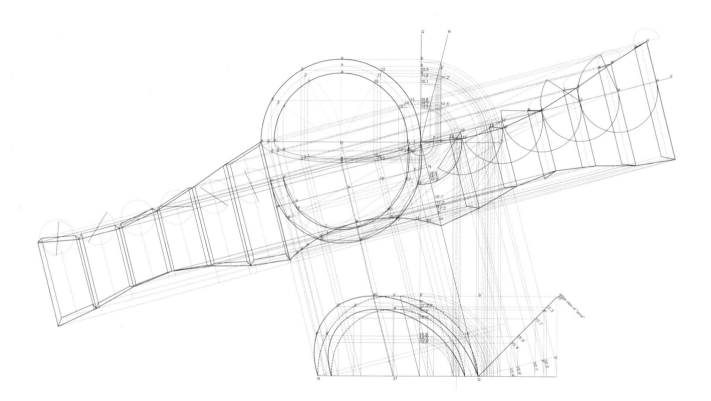

Fig 2.4

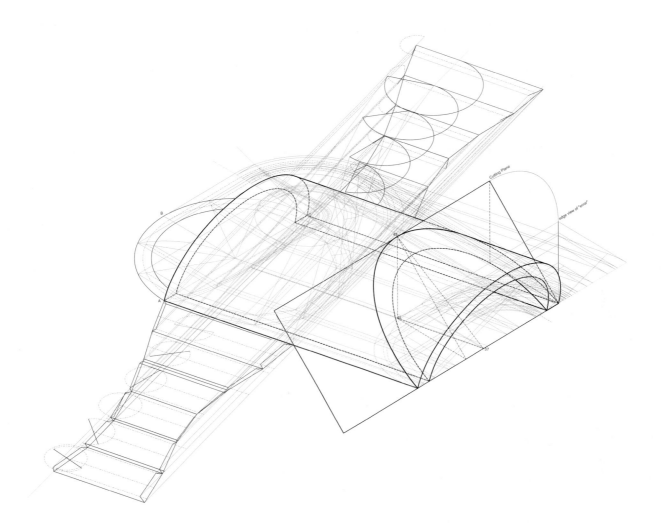

Fig 2.5

posthumous *Architettura civile* with a similar drawing from Guarini's earlier treatise on Euclidean geometry, *Euclides adauctus et methodicus mathematicaeque universalis* (1671),[13] showing that the earlier treatise, completed during Guarini's lifetime, solved a similar problem correctly. Thus, according to Müller, the error indicates that someone other than Guarini completed the text and drawing in *Architettura civile*: "Vittone, who designed such notable work as the Cappella della Visitazione in Vallinotto at about the same time as the publication of Guarini's *Architettura civile*, would, according to this, be so little acquainted with the fundamentals of the traditional methods of stonecutting, that he was unable to detect any erroneous exposition of stereotomic methods. That is the least conclusion that we can draw from our considerations."[14]

Müller noted two specific errors in *Architettura civile*: the first involves the dimensions of an ellipse to unroll an asymmetrical curve; the second is the construction of a curve (*R,45,Q*) created by the intersection of an oblique cylinder and a plane (SEE FIGURE 2.3). Guarini textually introduced the second "error," offering a drawing of the "natural size" of the intersection of the cylinder with an oblique and inclined plane.[15] Müller argued that Guarini (or Vittone) intended to draw the true size and shape of the curve produced by cutting the oblique cylinder with a vertical plane—a section drawing—because the convention for producing a section drawing is to project the drawn object perpendicularly from the plane of intersection. Müller consequently revised Guarini's drawing by both describing and drawing the seemingly correct projection of the oblique cylinder cut by a vertical plane (FIGURE 2.4).[16]

Müller's modern redrawing is correct if we assume that Guarini (or Vittone) accidentally replaced perpendicular measure, a fundamental procedure of orthographic projection, with oblique measure. Indeed, constructing an elevation drawing perpendicular to its plane of intersection is a basic orthographic principal, and it seems unlikely that either Guarini or Vittone would have made this mistake because perpendicular measure is fundamental not only of stereotomy but also of architectural drawing in general.[17] Guarini used the typical orthographic method throughout the construction of the drawing, but when it came time to plot the "natural size" of curve *R,45,Q*, he left this method behind (FIGURE 2.5).[18] Instead of tediously constructing all the necessary views to draw the curve, Guarini returned to Euclid. His drawing method involves the use of lines and marks to generate form, but the marks themselves are not based on visual representations of the curve. The marks and lines are rather used to calculate the relationships between similar triangles. The curve was drawn

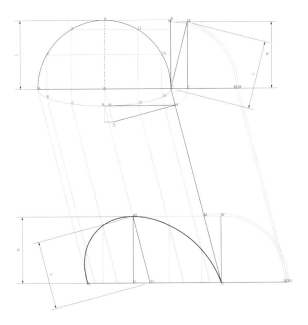

Fig 2.6

Fig 2.4
Reassembly of Guarino Guarini,
Architettura civile, Trattato IV, Lastra IV
A reassembled and extended version of Guarini's
original drawing, including the curve projection
proposed by Müller.

Fig 2.5
Three-Dimensional Illustration of Guarino Guarini,
Architettura civile, Trattato IV, Lastra IV
An illustration of the forty-five-degree plane implied
but not represented in Guarini's original.

Fig 2.6
Simplified Version of Guarino Guarini,
Architettura civile, Trattato IV, Lastra IV
Because the angle of inclination as defined by the line
MC relative to line *MT* is identical to the plan angle
defined by line *NS* relative to line *NH*, the triangles are
similar. When dimension *L* is transferred from line *MC* to
line *37,45*, the perpendicular line *45,V* to line *RQ* is equal
to the length of line *MT*. Because *MT* is the height of the
cylinder anywhere on line *37,0*, point *45* must be on the
surface of the cylinder on line *37,0*. This means that it is
displaced in plan (*45,V*) the exact amount it is displaced
in section (*MT*). It is located at the intersection of an
oblique cylinder and a plane with a slope of 1:1 or forty-
five degrees. A similar process can be used to locate
every point on curve *R,45,Q*.

correctly, but it was not drawn following modern principles of orthographic projection.

The Construction

The central object in the drawing is an oblique cylinder. A right cylinder, such as a standard piece of pipe, is created by extruding a circle perpendicular to the plane on which the circle lies. Conversely, an oblique cylinder is created by extruding a circle at any angle that is not perpendicular to the plane on which the circle lies. The construction of Guarini's drawing is based on rotating a vertical semicircle until it is located on an inclined plane and then extruding it at the same angle horizontally. To do this, Guarini instructed the reader to set the oblique angle in plan by drawing a new line (*NP*) that is not parallel to the base line of the original semicircle (*CA*). Once this line is drawn, Guarini instructed the reader to use the same angle to rotate the semicircle onto an inclined plane (FIGURE 2.6). The result is an oblique cylinder that is generated by horizontally extruding a semicircle from an inclined plane. Müller deemed this process unnecessary and "misleading," arguing that the horizontal and vertical angles do not need to correlate and that the "*MT*, and hence the angle of inclination, can be chosen otherwise."[19] Again, Müller's statement is correct as it pertains to orthographic projection in general; an oblique cylinder can be constructed without Guarini's insistence on correlating the two angles. However, a more important question is to ask why Guarini would provide so much detail on this operation if it were unnecessary. It seems far more likely that Guarini set these angles for a specific reason—a reason that becomes evident upon closer inspection of the drawings.

The first step in understanding the construction of this curve is solved by drawing a view of the oblique cylinder parallel to line *RQ*. Guarini did not construct this view and because his process made it unnecessary. The projection provides a side view of the intersection, showing that Guarini's plotted curve lies on a plane that cuts the cylinder at exactly forty-five degrees (SEE FIGURES 2.4, 2.5). Guarini's instructions plotted the points in the top view without the aid of a second view to project from, and yet they result in a planar cut through the cylinder at exactly forty-five degrees—an angle that is difficult to achieve accidentally. This is the first indication that something other than modern orthographic projection is at work in the drawing.

A diagonal line drawn between two opposite vertices in a square is at forty-five degrees. Because all sides of a square are equal, the two lines that intersect either vertex are also equal. In an orthographic projection, this means that the plan of a square is the same as its elevation. It also means that the top view of the diagonal line passing through the square is equal to both the square's plan and elevation (FIGURE 2.7). This is why Guarini's projection works. The inclined plane is at forty-five degrees; therefore, its top view is equal to its front view (i.e., its height) (FIGURE 2.8). This means that the height of any point on this curve is equal to its perpendicular displacement in plan, which solves most of the problem, except for the fact that Guarini did not plot the points on lines perpendicular to line *RQ*. He plotted them on oblique lines. However, this also works because Guarini set the oblique angle in the plan equal to the oblique angle in section. This action, which Müller deemed unnecessary, allowed Guarini to locate the curve in top view without the need for additional projections.

The operation is enabled by the construction of similar triangles, allowing Guarini not only to measure and construct a precise cut through an oblique cylinder but also to do so with a minimum of drawing. To explain this, the drawing has been simplified (SEE FIGURE 2.6). Line *CB* is the total height of semicircle *ABC*. All points on the semicircle are projected onto line *CB* and then rotated until they intersect line *CM*. Line *CM* is therefore equal in length to line *CB*, but it is now oriented at an angle. It is also the orientation of the plane onto which semicircle *ABC* has been rotated. The top view of the reoriented semicircle is denoted by curve *A,23,C*. Line *MT* is equal to the new height of the semicircle above the ground plane. The angle relative to line *CB* has been set at exactly the same angle as line *CS* in plan, per Guarini's instructions.[20] Line *CS* sets the orientation of the plan extrusion, so all the lines extending between curve *A,23,B* and line *RQ* are parallel to line *CS*. These lines lie on the surface of the oblique cylinder *ABRQ*. This means that the height of line *23,37* is exactly the same above the ground as line *MT*. Furthermore, when Guarini instructed the reader to transfer distance *CB* to line *23,37* and locate point *45*, he was instructing the reader to construct the right triangle *J,45,37*. Because line *37,45* is the same length as line *CM*, line *J,45* is the same length as line *MT*. This means that if point *45* were moved in space vertically the exact same distance as its position in plan denoted by line *J,45*, it would intersect the oblique cylinder on line *37,23*.

Repeating this operation at every point on curve *R,45,Q* will result in the production of a series of similar triangles, all of which locate points on a forty-five-degree plane that cuts through the oblique cylinder. Granted, Guarini never drew or referred to a forty-five-degree plane, but following his instructions yields the results evident in

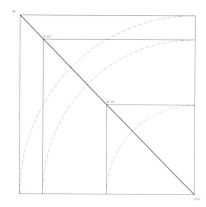

Fig 2.7

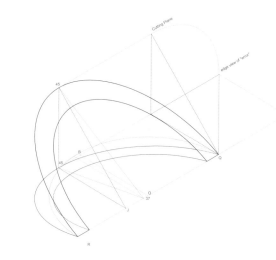

Fig 2.8

Fig 2.7
Squares of Curve *R,45,Q*
Because each point on curve *R,45,Q* is displaced in plan the same amount it is in section, curve *R,45,Q* lies on a plane that bisects a square. This plane is at forty-five degrees.

Fig 2.8
Plotting of Curve *R,45,Q* in Three Dimensions
Point *45* lies at the termination of a forty-five-degree triangle, with a base and height equal in length to line *J,45*.

FIGURE 2.6. Consequently, Müller was correct that Guarini's projection is not perpendicular and, therefore, is difficult to reconcile with the modern system of orthographic projection. In fact, Guarini's operation is not really a projection at all. Instead, he used the relationship between similar triangles and the properties of a forty-five-degree plane to locate points in space. For Guarini, this is part of the project of orthographic projection, which is why he included it in his treatise on the subject. It is a means of generating and measuring form without resorting to visual representation.

While there is no definitive means of proving that this was Guarini's method for deriving the curve, it does demonstrate that his drawing is geometrically correct. The curve that Guarini drew and described lies on the surface of the oblique cylinder. It would be hard to believe, given the specificity of Guarini's instructions on setting the angle of inclination, that this was an accident. To further complicate this, the operation directly following the drawing of the curve does not make use of any of the information derived from this curve. In other words, the operation translates the geometry of the drawing into instructions for the assembly of an object—a vault made of stones, but curve $R,45,Q$ is not part of this drawing and is consequently not part of the vault. In that sense, it is an additional (rather than incomplete) drawing that tells us more about the difference between Müller's analysis and Guarini's techniques then it does about any errors supposedly present in that drawing.

Before Convention

Descriptive geometry was not codified into a system of rule-based operations until 1795.[21] Guarini's text and Vittone's potential additions both predate this codification. A modern reader might then conclude that Guarini's instructions to project obliquely from the reference plane are not correct within the system of descriptive geometry or orthographic projection, but Guarini might have seen this "error" as an expedient and efficient means of solving a problem using both his knowledge of orthographic projection and Euclidean principles.[22] As we have seen, Müller's analysis was based on a modern position that understands orthographic projection as a system of representation defined by perpendicular views, whereas Guarini resorted to a range of geometric techniques that lie both within and beyond the modern system of orthographic projection. Thus, what Müller considered to be an error in Guarini's drawings was rather a malleable and adaptive set of geometric techniques—techniques that focus on the measurement and generation of form instead of the conventions of representation.[23] Formal analysis of Guarini's drawings reveals a disjunction between two drawing methods that share the same name, demonstrating that what architecture considers to be its most representative form of drawing, orthographic projection, has changed so substantially that modern orthographic projection cannot be used on its own to analyze its historic precedents. More importantly, this disjunction is an opportunity to reimagine orthographic projection, but to do so requires further inquiry into discrepancies between what constitutes an orthographic projection now and what it meant in the past.

1   Alberto Perez-Gomez, *Architecture and the Crisis of Modern Science* (Cambridge, MA: MIT, 1983), 279.
2   See Müller, "Authenticity of Guarini's Stereotomy."
3   See, e.g., Elwin C. Robison, "Optics and Mathematics in the Domed Churches of Guarino Guarini," *Journal of the Society of Architectural Historians* 50, no. 4 (December 1991): 384–401.
4   Guarini, *Architettura civile*, 191.
5   Martin Kemp, *The Science of Art: Optical Themes in Western Art from Brunelleschi to Seurat* (New Haven, CT: Yale University Press, 1990), 2.
6   Joseph Connors, "S. Ivo Alla Sapienza: The First Three Minutes," *Journal of the Society of Architectural Historians* 55, no. 1 (March 1996): 38–57, 41.
7   A clear example of this can be found in Rudolph Wittkower's analysis of Palladio's Villas. The 12th analytic diagram provides a new drawing that does not directly correspond to any of the Villas. It is a general type, and it is a new drawing that blurs the line between analysis and proposal. See Rudolf Wittkower, *Architectural Principles in the Age of Humanism*, 3rd ed. (London: Norton, 1962). 55–100, 73.
8   "*La qual Opera prevenuto dalla morte non avendo egli potuto mandare alla luce, ha lasciato a noi la fatica di ripulirla, e riunirla in un Volume nel che non poco ci ha sollevati il Signor Bernardo Vittone Architetto Accademico della insigne Accademia di S. Luca di Roma.*" See Guarini, *Architettura civile*, n.p.
9   Müller, "Authenticity of Guarini's Stereotomy." 206.
10   "*Il che ognuno potrà vedere leggendo l'Opera, che presentiamo all' universale profitto, acciocchè dall'Autore il principale intento s'adempia, a cui per quanto a noi su possibile, vi abbiamo posto, e attenzione, e studio, e diligenza.*" See Guarini, *Architettura civile*, n.p.
11   Ibid., 242.
12   Ibid., 244.
13   Guarino Guarini, *Euclides adauctus et methodicus mathematicaeque universalis* (Turin: B. Zavatta, 1671).
14   Müller, "Authenticity of Guarini's Stereotomy," 207.
15   Guarini, *Architettura civile*, 212.
16   Müller, "Authenticity of Guarini's Stereotomy," 205.
17   Consider Leon Battista Alberti's description of architectural drawing: "The architect...takes his projections from the ground plan and, without altering lines and by maintaining the true angles, reveals the extent and shape of each elevation and side." See Leon Battista Alberti, *The Art of Building in Ten Books*, trans. Joseph Rykwert, Neal Leach, and Robert Tavenor (Cambridge, MA: MIT Press, 1988), 34.
18   Guarini, *Architettura civile*, 212.
19   Müller, "Authenticity of Guarini's Stereotomy," 206.
20   Guarini, *Architettura civile*, 212.
21   Perez-Gomez, *Architecture and the Crisis of Modern Science*, 279.
22   It is also a technique that Guarini deployed throughout the fourth tractate. See the section "Euclid's Wedge" in the chapter "Reassembling Guarini."
23   Perez-Gomez, *Architecture and the Crisis of Modern Science*, 94.

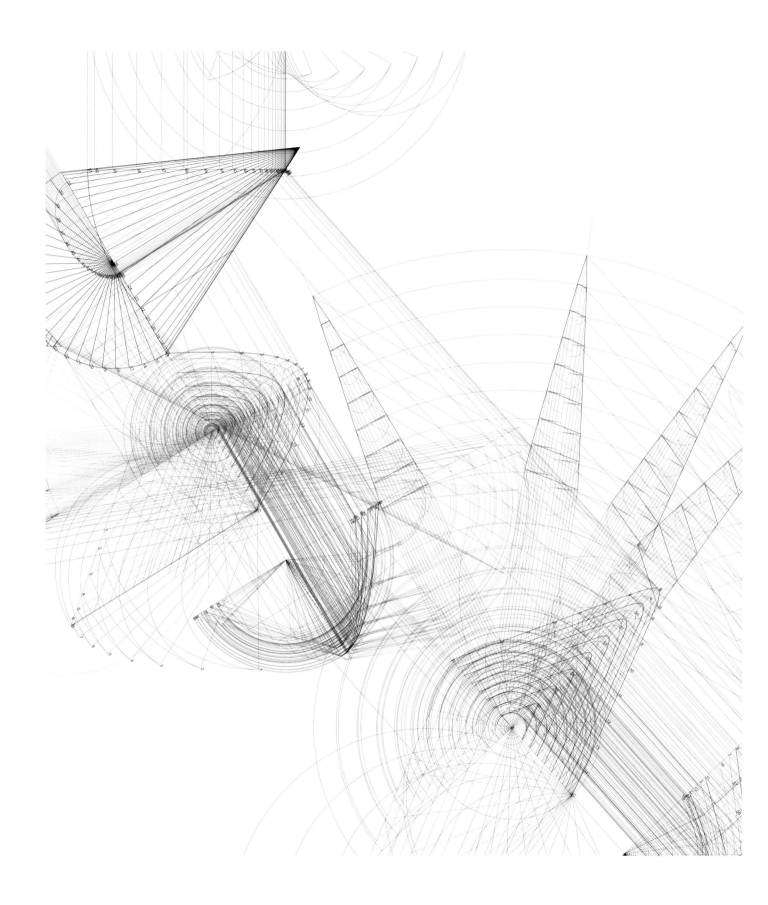

Reassembling Guarini

The role of history in the production of architecture has been and continues to be contested.[1] The 1990s brought a shift in architecture, as architects adopted digital tools to produce forms that could not have been designed otherwise.[2] The proximity of this work to the historical references of postmodernism created a difficult relationship between the implementation of new technologies and history.[3] Some architects reacting to postmodernism advocated for the direct engagement with technology in lieu of architectural history.[4] Others argued for connections between digital work and the history of geometry.[5] More recently, a number of architects and academics have turned toward history for ways to instigate new ideas relative to structure and form.[6] All these projects question whether historical techniques have a role in the development of new technological practices or whether they should be set aside.

Architectural drawing is at the center of this problem, as the historical conventions of plan, section, and elevation still dominate both practice and academia. Their conventional position has made them a commonplace digitization of a historical form of drawing. Originally the products of orthographic projection, these conventions are now encapsulated in software as default operations. Whereas historically the practice required the projection of information between two-dimensional drawings, the digital tools create innumerable views for a single three-dimensional digital model.[7] This separates the process of form generation (i.e., digital modeling) from the production of the orthographic drawing, leaving the latter

Opposite
Detail: Euclid's Hyperbolic Wedge

as little more than a disciplinary convention of representation. Once operating as the means by which architects both generate and describe form, orthographic projection now operates as a form of representation divorced from its procedural history. In this chapter I examine the procedural history of Guarini's orthographic projections, exposing aspects of the techniques that depart from the conventions of visual representation. These techniques, not their materialization in either pixels or ink, have future relevance in the development of architectural drawing.

Architettura civile

Robin Evans argued that only "two well-known architects" gave orthographic projection a "significant place in their writings— Phillibert Delorme and Guarino Guarini" and that this aspect of their work has largely been ignored.[8] The fourth tractate of *Architettura civile*, called "Dell'ortografia gettata," is devoted entirely to the explanation of the methods to create drawings for stonecutting templates from an array of three-dimensional surfaces. Importantly, Guarini's tractate on orthographic projection precedes the documentation of his architecture in plan, section, and elevation. Thus, while the treatise describes both Guarini's built and proposed architectural projects, it does not make a clear connection between the drawing techniques described in "Dell'ortografia gettata" and his architectural plans, sections, and elevations. How or if Guarini used these techniques in his own works is uncertain. Regardless, as Guarini noted in his introduction to the fourth tractate, his orthographic projections were unique to the Italian peninsula at the time.[9]

The drawings contained in "Dell'ortografia gettata" are obtuse and only partially figurative. Instead of representing views on an object, they represent the entirety of the geometric information described with as few lines as possible. Cones appear as right triangles in the unrolling of double-curved surfaces. Spheres appear as arcs, and top views of vaults are indistinguishable from their projection lines. To further complicate the reading of these drawings, they are organized to fit the maximum amount of drawings on a single sheet of paper. Thus, instead of being organized sequentially in the convention of a modern drawing set or an animation storyboard, they are organized like sardines in a can (FIGURE 3.1). This simple action removed the methodological evidence from the drawings that accompany the text, making Guarini's process nearly opaque. While examination of these drawings by someone familiar with descriptive geometry or orthographic projection will allow for a general understanding of their

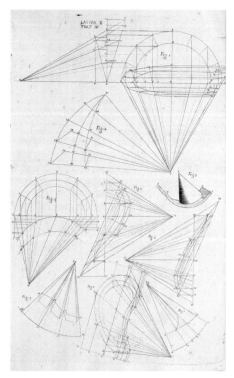

Fig 3.1

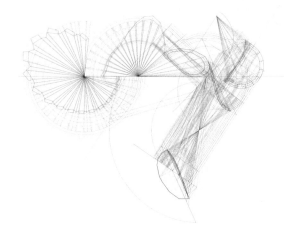

Fig 3.2

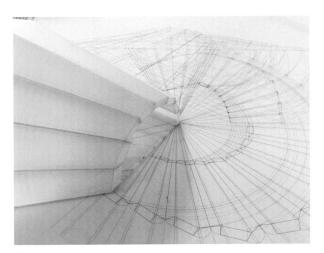

Fig 3.3

contents, they only become legible at a detailed level when cross-referenced with Guarini's text. This becomes even more evident upon inspection of the numbering in the drawings, which varies, making it difficult to track the position of a single point in multiple drawings because the points are renamed from drawing to drawing.[10]

Furthermore, Guarini's drawings do not adhere to the rules of modern orthographic projection. Guarini's drawings that appear to be orthographic projections may also include proportional operations and Euclidean constructions to bypass a large amount of actual projections. The evidence for these operations is located entirely in the text. Thus, deciphering Guarini's text and drawings requires the reassembly of each example into a single orthographic projection (FIGURES 3.2, 3.3). Each of the following explanations documents in text and drawing the methodological idiosyncrasies of Guarini's work. The drawings in this chapter do not repeat Guarini's originals but rather analyze and extend his methods to understand their mechanics, and and through them, I speculate on their contemporary resonance. Vittone may have set out to "clean" and "assemble" the drawings left in Guarini's incomplete manuscript,[11] but the following work seeks an alternative trajectory for orthographic projection through a reassembling of Guarini's techniques.

Euclid's Wedge[12]

Inasmuch as an orthographic drawing provides an abstract view of an architectural object that is both visible and measurable, it is useful because it allows important architectural elements—corners, windows, and doors—to be both visually recognized and located in space. While Guarini's drawings rely on this aspect of orthography as well, it is not the primary means of organization in "Dell'ortografia gettata." Instead, the drawings describe geometric objects—cones, spheres, and cylinders—by delineating only their fundamental geometric properties. Cones are represented as triangles and spheres as circles. While these figures do not fully visualize the geometric objects, they do provide all the necessary information to measure it.

Guarini also moved beyond this strategy for orthographic projection. In the seventh chapter of the fourth tractate, Guarini introduced a drawing type unlike all his previous examples. Each chapter in the tractate explicates a specific class of geometries. The second observation of chapter seven focuses on ellipsoid vaults, which introduces a new form of complexity.[13] A vault derived from spherical geometry has identical sections through both 90 and 180 degrees of rotation. This allows a circular plan to generate the section without additional information (FIGURE 3.4). Practically, this means that a spherical dome can be generated from an arch, making its construction a direct and repeatable operation.[14] Conversely, the ellipsoidal section is not identical through rotation. A simple solution to this is to rotate the ellipse ninety degrees relative to either its minor or major axis, generating an ellipsoid. However, this provides for only two possible ellipsoidal domes for any given elliptical plan. It is highly limiting and does not account for the wide variety of both elliptical and oval domes that were constructed in the seventeenth century.[15] To overcome this problem, Guarini adopted a form of visual calculation that operates both independent of and in conjunction with an orthographic projection.

Guarini's technique is almost invisible at first glance. The drawing construction appears to be organized as two views of a vault, with one view reflected downward and rotated approximately thirty degrees (FIGURE 3.5). The most significant component of the drawing is located in the triangular space between the reflected and rotated drawings. Within this triangular wedge of space is situated a set of parallel lines drawn over a set of converging lines. The drawing at the top of the construction is a cross section through the dome. The rotated and reflected drawing is an overlay of a horizontal section through the dome and a semicircle from which all the geometry is derived. The first part of the operation involves transforming the upside-down semicircle into a semiellipse by means of projecting it across two nonparallel lines. This is a familiar orthographic operation, which is often tied to the view of a semicircle projected onto an inclined plane (FIGURE 3.6). This standard explanation ties the abstract process of orthographic projection to the visual results of an intersection, moving it from the abstract to the perceptual. But Guarini did not tie his drawing to vision. Instead, he referenced Euclid, which allowed him not only to proportionally deform a circle into an ellipse but also to generate the entire surface of the ellipsoid.[16] The key figure to this transformation is the wedge of lines situated between the two orthographic drawings.

In his recent work, Bernard Cache pointed to several figures within Dürer's treatise, *Intsruction in Measurement*, that he described as "parametric."[17] One figure, similar to Guarini's wedge, is a triangle used to develop variable configurations of curves, lines, and the human body (FIGURE 3.7). For Cache, this figure is an example of parametric design because of its ability to produce variable outcomes.[18] Furthermore, while much of Cache's work focuses on the description and parametric modeling of the instruments that Dürer developed to create curves, this is the only example of a drawing capable of

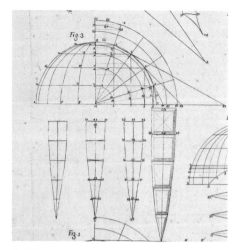

Fig 3.4

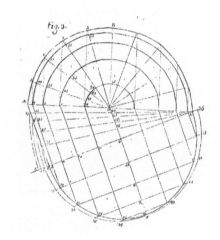

Fig 3.5

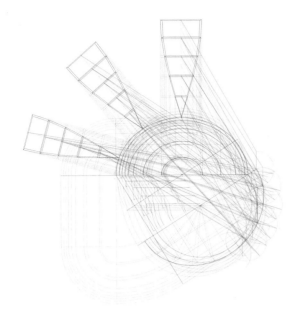

Fig 3.6

Fig 3.4
Reconstruction of Guarino Guarini, *Architettura civile*,
Trattato IV, Lastra XIII, Figura 3
This reconstruction demonstrates that a spherical vault
can be generated from a single semicircle. All information necessary for the drawing can be extracted from the
semicircle through orthographic projection.

Fig 3.5
Guarino Guarini, *Architettura civile*,
Trattato IV, Lastra XIV, Figura 3
This is Guarini's solution for an ellipsoidal dome. At the
center of the construction is a wedge of lines. This triangular space is where Guarini inserted Euclid's intercept
theorem and calculated all the curvature of the dome
without visual representation of the dome itself.

Fig 3.6
Reconstruction of Guarino Guarini, *Architettura civile*,
Trattato IV, Lastra XIV, Figura 3
The reconstruction of Guarini's solution for ellipsoidal
domes with the templates unrolled.

calculating form solely through the use of a compass and ruler.[19] A similar figure appears in the Juan Caramuel y Lobkowitz *Architectura civil recta y obliqua* (1678) (FIGURE 3.8).[20] In Caramuel's and Dürer's treatises, the figure operates in isolation as a means of calculating proportional relationships.[21] However, in Guarini's *Architettura civile*, the figure is wedged into the workings of an orthographic projection. Its position within the drawing is not simply convenient; it is also generative.

Guarini stated that we know this figure from "our Euclid."[22] His statement leads to a discourse on ellipsoid sections from his Latin treatise on geometry, *Euclides adauctus*. Further examination reveals that although Guarini used the wedge to accurately describe the proportional relationship between the changing curvatures on the surface of ellipsoid vaults, the figure itself has little if any direct relationship with an ellipse. Furthermore, the wedge's use in both Dürer's and Caramuel's text suggests another origin—one that is not explicitly linked to ellipses. Dürer used the wedge to develop forti-fications, as Cache noted, and to develop measuring lines for the proportional construction of the human figure.[23] Caramuel used the wedge to calculate proportional relationships between converging lines.[24] In these cases, it was used to construct variable measurements along curved and straight lines. Thus, Guarini used the wedge solely for the purpose of calculating the distance from the center of the ellipse to points on the surface of a smoothly curving ellipsoid. It is not a drawing of any part of the ellipse. Rather, it calculates variable distances from a common point and was used not as a form of visual-ization but as a form of calculation.

A closer examination of Guarini's drawing practice demonstrates the drawings' precise computational mechanics (FIGURES 3.9–3.11). His construction begins with the striking of two nonparallel lines that converge at a point in the drawing (SEE FIGURE 3.6). One line is equal to the major diameter of the ellipse, the other to the minor diameter. A line is then drawn to connect the end points of both lines. Additional lines are constructed parallel to this new line from each of the orthographic projectors at the points on the original ellipse. Ignoring the ellipse for the moment, we can see that the relationship between the two nonparallel lines and the parallel lines is central. The parallel lines divide the intersecting lines into proportional segments. Repeating this process with all the projectors of the ellipse and transferring them to the polar grid defined by the ellipse's center will produce a series of curves. The curves are transverse sections through the ellipsoid vault, and although in this case the drawing

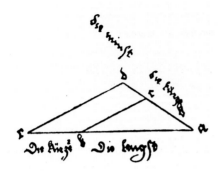

Fig 3.7

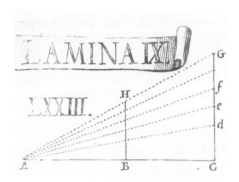

Fig 3.8

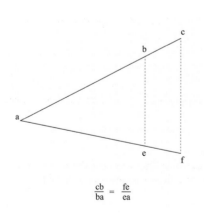

$$\frac{cb}{ba} = \frac{fe}{ea}$$

Fig 3.12

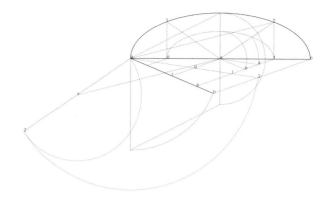

Fig 3.9

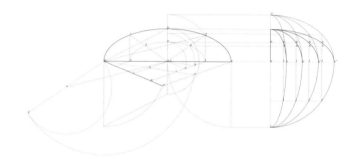

Fig 3.10

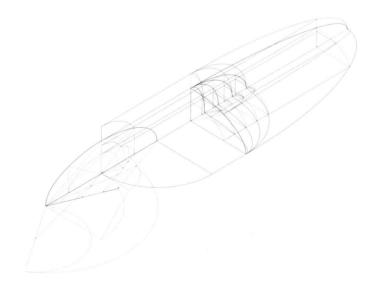

Fig 3.11

Fig 3.13

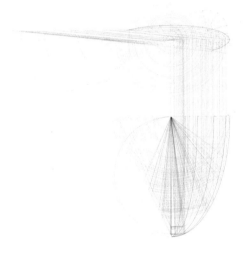

Fig 3.14

Fig 3.15

Fig 3.7
Albrecht Dürer, *Painter's Manual*
Dürer's drawing of Euclid's intercept theorem.

Fig 3.8
Juan Caramuel y Lobkowitz, *Architectura civil recta y obliqua*
Caramuel's drawing of Euclid's intercept theorem.

Fig 3.9
Euclid's Wedge Explained
The first semiellipse (*ABC*) is the starting point. The second semiellipse (*DEF*) is derived from the wedge-shaped figure beneath it. Minor radius *XB* is doubled to produce line *AM*. Line *AM* can be rotated to any angle as long as it is not parallel to line *AB*. A line is then drawn from point *M* to point *C*. The angle of this line is used to construct a series of parallel lines extending from points *F*, *X*, and *D* to line *AM*. Next, line *X2* is doubled to produce the diameter at this point in the ellipse. It is then rotated until it intersects line *BC* at point *N*. Line *AN* is then divided by the parallel lines extending from points *D*, *X*, and *F* to line *AB*. These new divisions provide a proportional calculation of a new curve (*D,E,F*) plotted from point *X*. Therefore, distance *QL* is a proportional variant of distance *X2*. Because the ellipse is bilaterally symmetrical, transferring distance *QL* to lines *X2* and *X1* will locate points *3* and *4*, respectively, on curve *DEF*.

Fig 3.10
Euclid's Wedge and Multiple Vaults
In this version, the first semiellipse (*ABC*) is used to generate a series of different longitudinal sections based on the same calculations from the wedge. Guarini's technique allows for the production of multiple vaults from a single source curve.

Fig 3.11
Euclid's Wedge and Multiple Forms
A three-dimensional illustration of the previous drawing.

Fig 3.12
Euclid's Intercept Theorem
The length of lines *AC* and *AF* differ, but they are related proportionally through parallel lines.

Fig 3.13
Euclid's Wedge Alone
Two sets of lines are intersected based on the dimensions of a single curve. The true measurements of every section through the ellipsoid are contained in the grid.

Fig 3.14
Euclid's Wedge within an Orthographic Projection
The dimensions from the wedge of lines are then transferred into a polar grid via orthographic projection to describe the true shape of every section precisely.

Fig 3.15
Euclid's Hyperbolic Wedge
This drawing tests the wedge against all conic sections. Each drawing extracts a single conic section from the same cone and then uses Euclid's wedge to calculate the dimensional information of a series of vaults.

process has been inserted into an orthographic projection, it is not a projection itself.

The wedge was not derived from orthographic projection. Instead, it originated in Euclid's *Elements* (ca 300 BCE). In the second proposition of book six, Euclid stated, "If a straight line be drawn parallel to one of the sides of a triangle, it will cut the sides of the triangle proportionally."[25] This statement, absent of references to ellipses, is the generator of the wedge. The proposition, described as the "intercept theorem," establishes a proportional relationship between nonparallel lines via the use of parallel projectors.[26] It also establishes a process in which any set of two or more lines can be proportionally divided (FIGURE 3.12). If we take this process and begin with the minor and major axes of an ellipse, we can see that this proportional relationship will provide the same result as the one offered by Guarini for the development of ellipsoid vaults. The form of the ellipsoid, and all subsequent drawings generated to develop stonecutting templates, are a product of Euclidean principles wedged into the space between two orthographic projections (FIGURES 3.13, 3.14). The drawing practice can be extended to produce the vaults of any conic section (FIGURE 3.15)—a seventeenth-century drawing technique that has been used to compute form and dimension without the aid of references to perceptual space (FIGURES 3.16).

Fig 3.16

Strong Card[27]

In the ninth observation of chapter three in the fourth tractate, Guarini described the process of obtaining the drawings for a vault that intersects a cylinder at an oblique angle (FIGURE 3.17).[28] Through text and drawings, he explained the means by which the oblique angle of intersection is configured in three views. Guarini then left the parallel lines behind and introduced a new drawing technique. He began by describing the oblique section of a cylinder as an ellipse and referenced Euclid as his source for the information. He went on to explain that since we can measure the height and breadth of the ellipse in the orthographic drawings, we have the necessary information to construct an ellipse that would be the section through the cylinder at the plane of intersection with the vault.[29] At this point, Guarini developed an argument based on Euclid's propositions, and then he provided a template for the semiellipse and instructed the reader to make a drawing instrument out of a "strong card," using the template as a guide.[30]

This new instrument can be used to project points located on a baseline along the elliptical section of the cylindrical surface (FIGURE

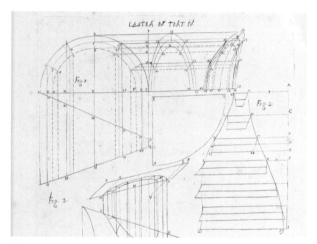

Fig 3.17

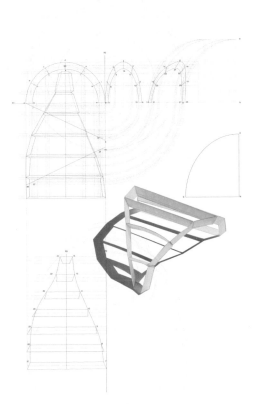

Fig 3.18

Fig 3.16
Euclid's Parabolic Wedge
This drawing begins with a parabola and uses the wedge
to generate the surface of the vault without constructing
a longitudinal section. The vault only appears as a set of
splayed sections and unrolled surfaces, none of which
are parallel.

Fig 3.17
Guarino Guarini, *Architettura civile*,
Trattato IV, Lastra IV, Figure 1–3
An elliptical template to resolve a cylindrical
intersection.

Fig 3.18
Reconstruction of Guarino Guarini, *Architettura civile*,
Trattato IV, Lastra IV, Figure 1–3
This reconstruction uses an elliptical template to
construct the projection. The paper model tests
the resolution.

3.18). Rather than projecting from the section and plan until a suffi-cient number of points of intersection can be obtained to approxi-mate the curves of intersection, Guarini adapted Euclid to create an instrument that draws curves specific to the geometric object under study. His drawing method adapts and responds to the task at hand, generating elliptical intersections that are not approximations but rather precisely related to the curvature of the cylinder. Thus, it is not a general method of architectural representation. It is a case-specific method that has been formed through an innovative redeployment of mathematical principles nearly two thousand years old.

The difficulty of drawing a line at an oblique angle along a cylindrical surface is not a technical challenge within our current instrumental framework. Current practices offer an array of tools by which complex curved surfaces can be analyzed, measured, and built. However, in many cases these techniques result in the produc-tion of lines that are not directly related to the specific geometry of the surface. Instead, they are the result of a standardized tool kit of form descriptions. The lines represent the intersection of a surface with an abstract blade that has only a coincidental relationship with the surface, or they are simply engendered by the computational bias of a command within a given software.[31] Alternately, host surfaces are used as the receptors of subdivisions with an individual order not tied to the figure's geometry. Had Guarini located the points of the inter-section between the vault and the oblique cylinder by orthographically projecting the vertical and horizontal points until they intersected and then plotted the curve, he would have followed a standardized route in which the logic of drawing was independent of the geometry of the figure.[32] Instead, he used the geometric properties of cylinders as a drawing instrument capable of describing forms more complex than the cylinder.

Guarini's method temporarily abandons the framework of the drawing to construct a template that is not a view of the object but a guide. The template is constructed by applying principles of geometry in the abstract. Guarini described his logic and proof of the geometric principles underlying his template in the text, but he did not prove it through graphic means.[33] The most important part of the drawing technique is not a view of the object at all; it is a template produced from a strong card.

Geometric Composites

The eighth chapter of the fourth tractate contains only one observa-tion: the unrolling of the surface of a torus, which Guarini referred to as an annulus (FIGURE 3.19).[34] A torus is a double-curved surface that cannot be unrolled onto a plane. Because orthographic drawing is contingent upon the positioning of true lengths parallel to the picture plane, double-curved surfaces present a specialized problem. Their dimensions cannot be flattened onto the picture plane. Thus, to produce the toroidal vault, Guarini combined the geometric properties of the torus with those of a cone to produce a third, nameless figure that can be unrolled.

Guarini described the torus in section as a semicircle of five segments. He then generated the top view of the toroidal vault by rotating the interior and exterior divisions of the semicircle about 180 and 90 degrees, respectively. Next, he intersected the generating semicircle of the torus with a series of cones, each with a triangular profile tangent to a chord in the subdivision of the semicircle. In the included reconstructed drawing, a semicircle is divided into eight segments so that a total of thirty-two cones are used to describe joints on the interior and exterior surface of the vault (FIGURE 3.20). Once the intersections of the cones and the torus are located, each of the cones is unrolled to generate the templates for stonecutting. The figure generated is neither a torus nor a cone; it is rather a combination of points on the surface of the torus and surface patches from thirty-two cones. This new figure is a composite geometry rendered through a set of logical arguments. It builds from the approximation of a curve with line segments to the approximation of a double-curved surface with patches of a developable surface—a cone.

Today, a similar process is called geometric approximation or optimization, as a more complex figure is approximated through the use of simpler geometric figures.[35] A three-dimensional model of the double-curved surface is created, and then the surface is approximated with another, simpler geometric figure, such as a triangle. However, as we have seen, in Guarini's example a torus is never drawn, neither is a cone. Instead, their geometric properties are intersected to produce a new figure. Each geometric object is represented with the minimum amount of information necessary to understand its three-dimensional properties and to translate them into measurements. The most significant graphic outputs of the drawing are the unrolled stones of the vault. In a digital modeling environment, the vault would first be rendered as a three-dimensional model and then unrolled. In this example, the vault is not drawn as an object but rather as a set of related geometric properties that are only translated into legible objects as the unrolled templates. The templates for the thick and heavy stone material have been drawn from a set of profile lines without thickness or apparent object qualities.

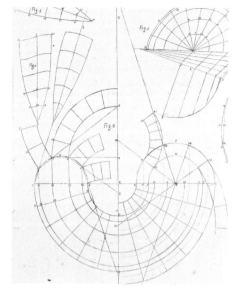

Fig 3.19

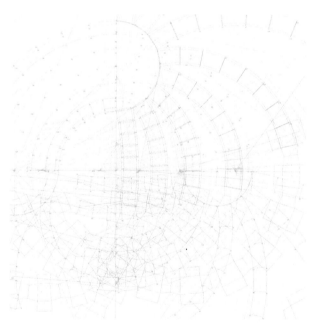

Fig 3.20

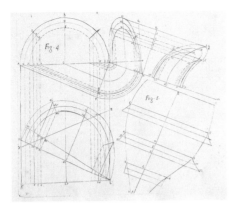

Fig 3.21

Fig 3.19
Guarino Guarini, *Architettura civile*,
Trattato IV, Lastra XIV, Figura 8
Guarini's development of a torus by intersecting it with
a series of cones.

Fig 3.20
Reconstruction of Guarino Guarini, *Architettura civile*,
Trattato IV, Lastra XIV, Figura 8
For the reconstruction of Guarini's development of a
toroidal vault, each point of convergence is the vertex of
an unrolled cone.

Fig 3.21
Guarino Guarini, *Architettura civile*,
Trattato IV, Lastra IV, Figure 4, 5
For Guarini's drawing of the intersection of a cone and a
barrel vault, the cone is delineated by its profile line (*AZ*)
and its axis (*KL*).

Reversibility

Reversibility is a key technical operation in Guarini's work. Almost all of Guarini's examples begin with a semicircle. The semicircle is projected onto various figures to produce vaults with complex curved profiles. The end figure of the operation is more complex than the starting point, and to overcome this complexity, Guarini relied on orthography's reversibility as a means of controlling the complex results of his drawing operations. For example, in observation thirteen of chapter three in the fourth tractate, Guarini provided instructions for the development of a semicylindrical barrel vault that is truncated by an oblique plane on one end and a cone on the other end (FIGURE 3.21).[36]

The drawing begins with the semicircle and through a set of operations that involve shifting the axis of the projection so that it is oriented to the oblique plane. The original, subdivided semicircular arch is distorted into two distinct curves: one curve is the intersection with an oblique plane; the other is the intersection with a cone. Once each of these curves had been plotted in side view, Guarini returned to the original semicircle as the dimensional control for unrolling the figure. The two distorted projections of the original semicircle appear as curves in the side view. Furthermore, the original semicircle is represented as a straight line. Guarini then unrolled the representative straight line of the semicircle by cross-referencing it with equal divisions of the original semicircle. Because parallel lines connect all three curves, the unrolling of the original curve also results in the unrolling of the more complex projective deformations. Guarini then reversed the projection, returning to the starting point so that the more complex result could be rationalized. Ultimtately, this is a practical operation that links an easily measured and known figure to a more complex and harder-to-measure deformation (FIGURE 3.22).

Ink, Paper, and Stone

Guarini used the term orthographic projection to describe the work of the fourth tractate.[37] While many of the drawings in *Architettura civile* are orthographic, there are no building plans or sections in the fourth tractate. This is due to the fact that the tractate deals largely with the production of the drawings of the individual stones that come together to produce a vault. And although Guarini did not use the term, this practice was sometimes referred to as stereotomy, starting in 1644.[38]

The objective of stereotomic drawing is to produce form by providing the dimensions to cut a heavy volumetric material.

Conversely, the design practice centers on the projection of drawings and light paper models. Three different materials must be engaged: ink, paper, and stone. The two materials that receive the gestural marks to translate drawing to object possess extremely different properties: paper can be folded and stone can be carved. This means that a different type of geometry must be deployed in each case. The drawings for paper use lines, and the drawings for stones use curves. Stereotomy not only defines the measurements of an object but also embeds the properties of a construction material in the form of the drawing.

In the fifth observation of chapter five in the fourth tractate, Guarini described the process of obtaining the unrolled surface of a spherical dome cut by a quadrangle.[39] The process involves the intersection of the dome's sphere with a developable surface and the repetition of a rectangular patch of the dome about the center (FIGURE 3.23). However, in the text describing the operation, Guarini made a point about the type of drawing and its purpose: "this is the method of dressing a sphere in a pliable surface, such as paper, or similar material, but it is our intention to teach the method of cutting stone to serve for the making of vaults, arches, and similar marvelous things."[40] The text and methodology in the example is thus for the construction of a spherical vault on paper (e.g., a card), but the purpose of the text is to teach the drawing of stonecutting templates for the construction of vaults (FIGURE 3.24). Guarini connected a type of drawing with a specific material. Paper models must be developable and require the use of straight lines at moments of folding. Stones do not fold and are instead carved using curves to more closely approximate the surface of a sphere. It is a simple observation that deploys seventeenth-century geometry and instrumentation to create drawings for specific materials—embedding the material properties of stone and paper in the shape of a line made in ink (FIGURE 3.25).

Currently, several scholars and architects examine stereotomy from the perspective of material construction. These studies tend to focus on the volumetric properties of stone and the structural qualities of vaulted architecture.[41] However, Guarini's text alludes not only to the importance of embedding the properties of the fabrication material in the geometric construction of the drawings but also to the potential for the drawing to impact the material form of the object. Examples of this are present throughout the text in a particular drawing type that shows the stones that compose the vault as if they were an unrolled three-dimensional solid (FIGURE 3.26).

In the sixth observation of chapter four in the fourth tractate, Guarini explained the process of unrolling a conoid.[42] A conoid is a

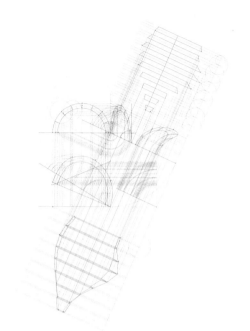

Fig 3.22

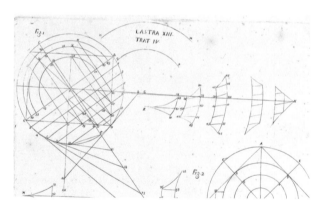

Fig 3.23

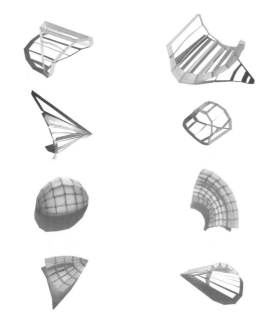

Fig 3.24

cone that terminates in a line in lieu of a point, and Guarini's process involves developing the conoid from a cone and then truncating it on a curved surface. However, it also includes a drawing type that shows the stones of the conoid vault laid out on a flat plane as if they had been unfolded. Thus, this drawing, depicting stone, transposes the qualities of the paper model onto the drawing of stone.

On Measure

Within each of Guarini's observations, the abstraction of vision plays a role, but it is not the only role. The drawings produced as outcomes of the work are the unrolled surfaces of the vaults that can be used to fold paper or cut stone.[43] As we have seen, the observations communicate the measurements needed to produce the templates for stone-cutting and are not dependent on the production of complete views of objects. To that end, the observations include a mix of logical arguments, Euclidean principles, proportions, and orthographic projections. The drawings cannot be understood or proven independent of the text; the two modes of communication are contingent upon one another. Furthermore, the structure of the operations at work within the drawings begins to suggest an alternate reading of orthographic projection—one that moves orthographic projection outside the conventions of plan, section, and elevation, mobilizing within the technique a set of geometric operations that are continually adapted to both generate and measure form. Guarini's orthographic projections involve a set of geometric operations that do not simply precede contemporary digital processes; the operations are embedded within those processes. Orthographic projection may have originated as a practice tied to the making of marks on a planar surface (paper or stone), but its future relevance lies in the procedural geometry and rules that govern digital processes (FIGURE 3.27).

Fig 3.22
Reconstruction of Guarino Guarini, *Architettura civile*, Trattato IV, Lastra IV, Figure 4, 5
This reconstruction of Guarini's drawing hinges on its reversibility.

Fig 3.23
Guarino Guarini, *Architettura civile*, Trattato IV, Lastra XIII, Figura 1
Guarini's solution for a spherical dome cut by a quadrangle.

Fig 3.24
Models from Guarino Guarini, *Architettura civile*
Guarini referred to paper models in his text. These models test some of the observations through their assembly in vellum.

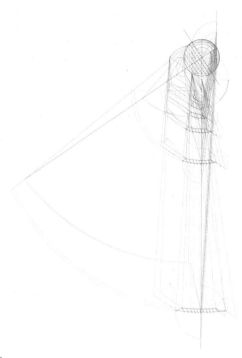

Fig 3.25

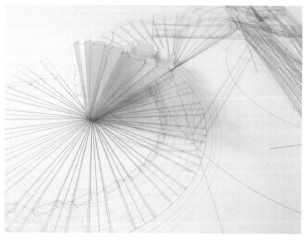

Fig 3.27

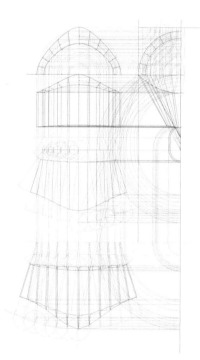

Fig 3.26

1   For more on this contested role, see, e.g., Manfredo Tafuri, "Operative Criticism," in *Theories and History of Architecture*, trans. Giorgio Verrecchia, 4th ed. (London: Harper and Row, 1980), 141–70.

2   For more on this shift, see, e.g., Carpo, *Digital Turn in Architecture*.

3   Greg Lynn, ed., *Archaeology of the Digital* (Montreal; Berlin: Canadian Centre for Architecture; Sternberg Press, 2013), 11.

4   Greg Lynn, *Animate Form* (New York: Princeton Architectural Press, 1999), 17–18.

5   Cache, "A Plea for Euclid," 32.

6   See, e.g., Mark Burry, "Geometry Working beyond Effect," *Architectural Design* 81, no. 1 (August 2011): 80–89.

7   May, "Everything Is Already an Image," 19.

8   Evans, *The Projective Cast: Architecture and Its Three Geometries*, xxiv–xxxv.

9   It is also on this page that Guarini credited the French for the development of orthographic projection, and he noted its relative absence in Italy at the time. See Guarini, *Architettura civile*, 191.

10 Müller argued that the discrepancies in numbering and other drawing errors may be a result of errors made during Vittone's production of *Architettura civile* from Guarini's incomplete manuscript. See Müller, "Authenticity of Guarini's Stereotomy," 207.

11 See the chapter "On Redrawing" for a reference to the use of the word "assembling" to describe Vittone's role in the completion of the manuscript.

12 An earlier version of this argument was published in Mark Ericson, "Euclid's Wedge," in *ACADIA 2014 Design Agency: Proceedings of the 34th Annual Conference of the Association for Computer Aided Design in Architecture*, ed. David Gerber and Alvin Huang (Cambridge, ON: Riverside Architectural Press, 2014), 125–34.

13 Guarini, *Architettura civile*, 260–62.

14 Santiago Huerta, "Oval Domes: History, Geometry and Mechanics," *Network Nexus Journal* 9, no. 2 (October 2007): 211–48.

15 The debate between oval and ellipse in Baroque church plans exceeds the scopes of this book. However, for a detailed analysis of the complexity involved in oval domes (and by extension elliptical domes) See Huerta, "Oval Domes," 237–39.

16 Guarini, *Architettura civile*, 261.

17 Bernard Cache, "Instruments of Thought: Another Classical Tradition," ed. Caroline O'Donnell, *Cornell Journal of Architecture*, no. 9 (2012)." 26.

18 To understand Cache's argument it is helpful to see the digital version of Dürer's instruments as Cache modeled them. See Bernard Cache, "Dürer-Vitruvius-Plato. Instruments of Thought" (April 2013), *https://www.youtube.com/watch?v=VxzdW4H4aww*.

19 Ibid.

20 Juan Caramuel Lobkowitz, *Architectura Civile Recta y Obliqua* (Vigevano: Camillo Corrado, 1678). Parte 2, Lamina 9.

21 Albrecht Dürer, *The Painter's Manual: A Manual of Measurement of Lines, Areas, and Solids by Means of Compass and Ruler*, trans. Walter Strauss (New York: Abaris, 1977).

22 Guarini, *Architettura civile*, 261.

23 Albert Dürer, *Della simmetria dei corpi humani* (Venice: Roberto Meietti, 1594), 2–4.

24 Lobkowitz does not provide a link to textual description of the figure in his list of illustrations, so this analysis is based on the figure alone. See Lobkowitz, *Architectura Civile Recta y Obliqua*, Parte 2, Lamina 9.

25 Euclid, *The Thirteen Books of Euclid's Elements*, trans. Thomas Heath (n.p.: Digireads.com, 2010), 100.

26 J. V. Field and J. J. Gray, *The Geometrical Work of Girard Desargues* (New York: Springer Verlag, 1987), 5.

27 An earlier version of this argument was published in Mark Ericson, "Manufacturing Method: A Study of the Stereotomic Methods of Guarino Guarini," in *ACADIA 2013 Adaptive Architecture: Proceedings of the 33rd Annual Conference of the Association for Computer Aided Design in Architecture*, ed. Philip Beesley, Omar Khan, and Michael Stacey (Cambridge, ON: Riverside Architectural Press, 2013), 173–78.

28 Guarini, *Architettura civile*, 206–7.

29 Ibid., 230–34.

30 Ibid., 204–6.

31 George Liaropoulos-Legendre, *ijp: The Book of Surfaces* (London: AA, 2002), 3, 0.

32 Robert Woodbury, in his important text on parametric design, covered the standard solution for sectioning a cylinder. Crucially, his method is the modern version contingent on the production of views of a cylinder. Guarini's is not. See Robert Woodbury, *Elements of Parametric Design* (Oxford: Routledge, 2010).

33 Guarini, *Architettura civile*, 204–6.

34 Ibid., 264–65.

35 Lisa Iwamoto, *Digital Fabrications: Architectural and Material Techniques* (New York: Princeton Architectural Press, 2009), 36.

36 Guarini, *Architettura civile*, 214–17.

37 Guarini, *Architettura civile*, 191.

38 Fallacara, "Digital Stereotomy and Topological Transformations," 1075.

39 Guarini, *Architettura civile*, 250–53.

40 "che la maniera di vestire una superficie molle, cioè di carta, o di simile materia; però essendo la nosttra idea d'insegnare la maniera di tagliare le pietre, acciocchè servino per fare volte, archi e simili di maravigliosa…" Ibid., 252.

41 See, e.g., Rippmann, "Funicular Shell Design."

42 Guarini, *Architettura civile*, 230–34.

43 Ibid.

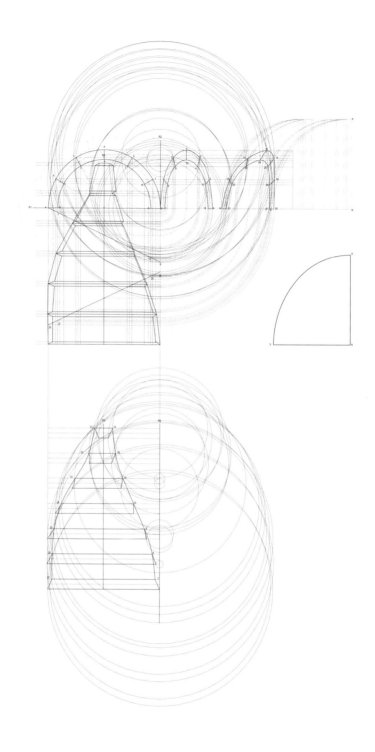

Fig 4.1
Trattato IV, Lastra IV, Figure 1–3

Guarini Reassembled

COLLECTION OF EIGHTEEN DRAWINGS

The drawings contained in this section are a product of the research described in the chapter "Reassembling Guarini." Each drawing was made by working from a facsimile of a Guarini original in *Architettura civile*. The focus of the research was on a single tractate, "Dell'ortografia gettata," in which Guarini explained a series of orthographic projections through individual observations. Guarini's text and drawings presented problems of interpretation and translation. On the one hand, the text, hundreds of years old and in Italian, includes words and phrases that even after translation are difficult to position in the drawings. Similarly, as established in the chapter "On Redrawing," the drawing techniques precede the codification of descriptive geometry and orthographic projection. They were made using an unfamiliar geometric language. This meant that although manuals on descriptive geometry help with some aspects of the drawings, other aspects could only be solved by tracking Guarini's descriptions back to Euclid. In addition, Guarini's drawings are scattered across the plates of *Architettura civile*. A single observation might contain four drawings, none of which align or share the same notation. The process of studying his drawings involves working between text and drawings to reassemble each observation into a single orthographic projection. Thus, in many cases, the accuracy of these projections was tested with the construction of paper models, per Guarini's instructions.

In the figure captions of this book, the drawings are titled by their original notation in *Architettura civile*. The original drawings are found at the end of the treatise in a series of unpaginated plates—"lastra"

(singular), "*lastre*" (plural) in Italian—that correspond with a tractate—"*trattato*" in Italian—with individual figures—"*figura*" (singular), "*figure*" (plural) in Italian. Therefore, "Trattato IV, Lastra X, Figure 4–8," is both a title and citation, allowing the reader of this book to locate the original drawings easily. The exception to this are the drawings that begin with the title "Euclid's Wedge." Each of these drawings was part of a series of studies that grew out of the analysis of "Trattato IV, Lastra XIV, Figura 3," and was explained in detail in the section "Euclid's Wedge." These drawings test Guarini's technique against a series of geometric conditions. They are different from the drawings based closely on Guarini's originals in that they do not reference specific instructions or figures in Guarini's text. These drawings, although constructed through conventional drafting practices, are closely related to the drawings described in the chapter "Animating Guarini." They are primarily graphic calculations that only map to legible shapes once they have been plotted in an orthographic projection.

The drawings were constructed digitally using only lines and circles in an architectural drafting software.[1] Each projection adheres to the same two-dimensional plane that Guarini used in the originals. Three-dimensional digital modeling was not used, as it would have prevented the investigation of the idiosyncrasies of Guarini's techniques. The drawings are thus two-dimensional orthographic projections that use grayscale linework and a single color.

---

1   The drawings were made in McNeel's software, Rhinoceros (versions five and six), with the line weights and color set in Adobe Illustrator CC.

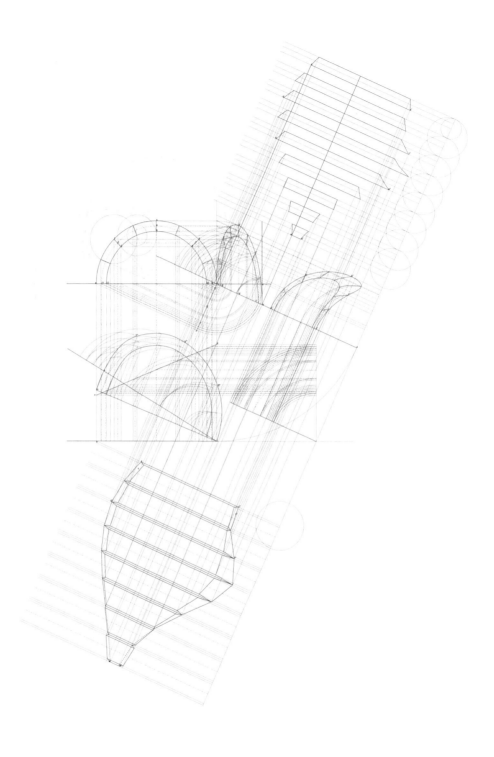

Fig 4.2
Trattato IV, Lastra IV, Figure 4–5

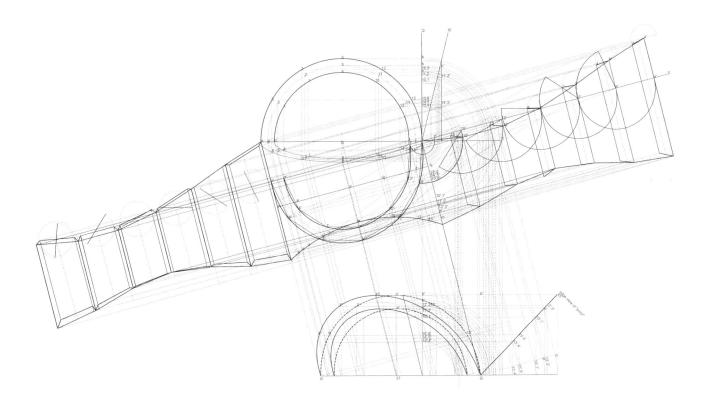

Fig 4.3
Trattato IV, Lastra VI, Figure 1–3

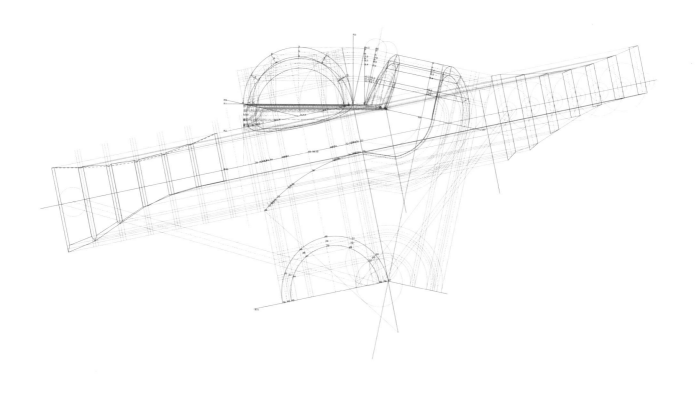

Fig 4.4
Trattato IV, Lastra VI, Figure 4–6

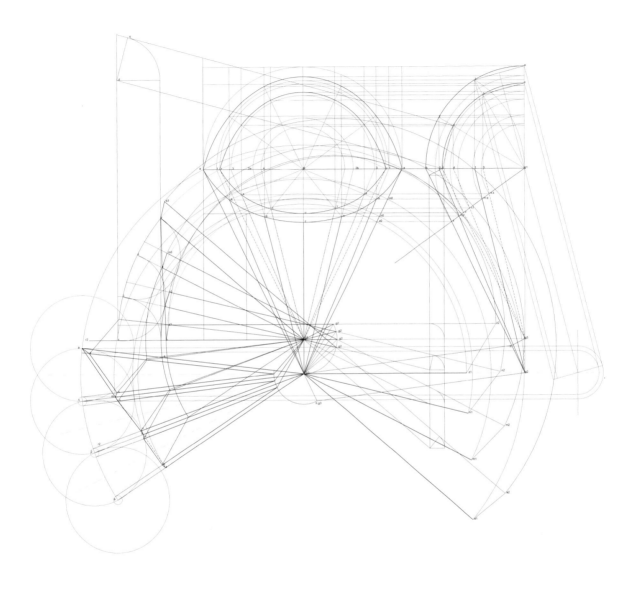

Fig 4.5
Trattato IV, Lastra VIII, Figure 3–6

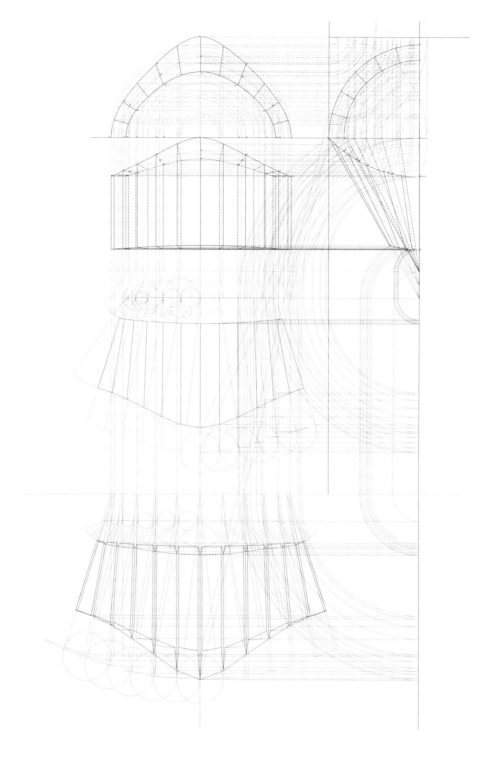

Fig 4.6
Trattato IV, Lastra IX, Figure 4–7

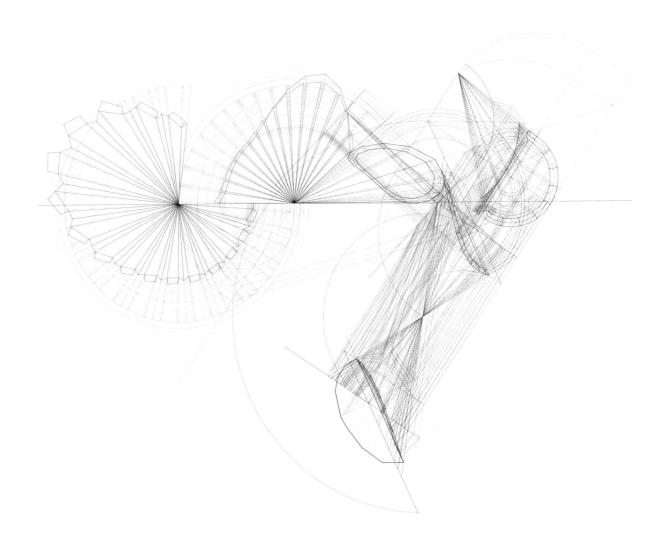

Fig 4.7
Trattato IV, Lastra X, Figure 4–8

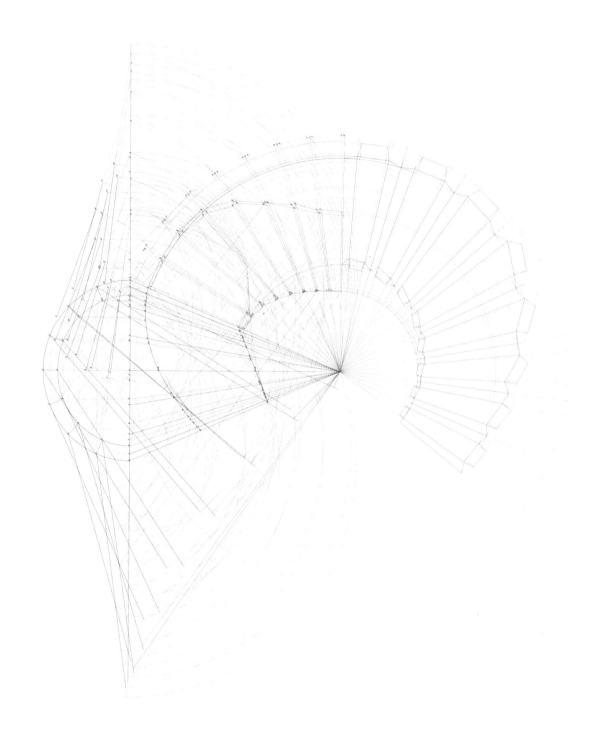

Fig 4.8
Trattato IV, Lastra XI, Figure 4–7

Fig 4.9
Trattato IV, Lastra XIII, Figura 1

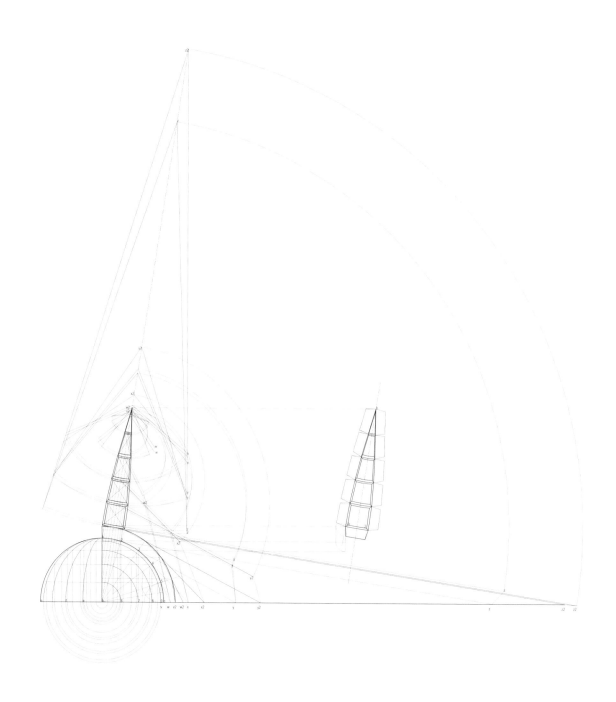

Fig 4.10
Trattato IV, Lastra XIII, Figura 3

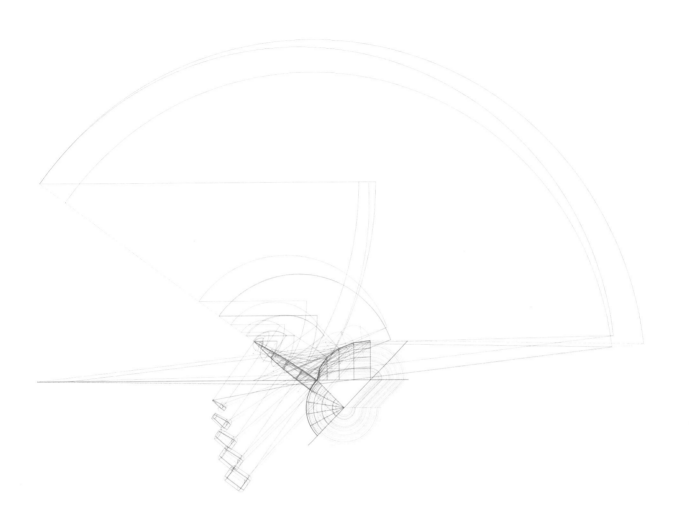

Fig 4.11
Trattato IV, Lastra XIV, Figure 1-2

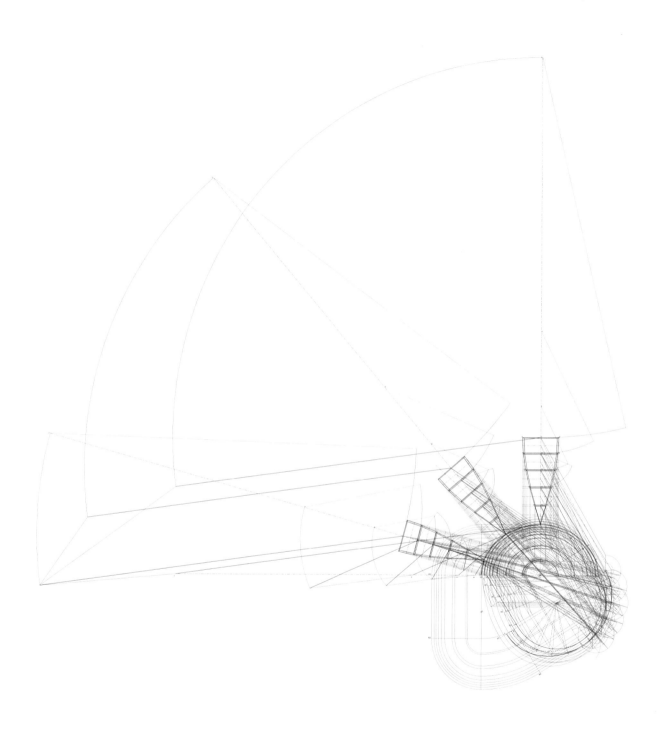

Fig 4.12
Trattato IV, Lastra XIV, Figura 3

Fig 4.13
Trattato IV, Lastra XIV, Figure 5–6

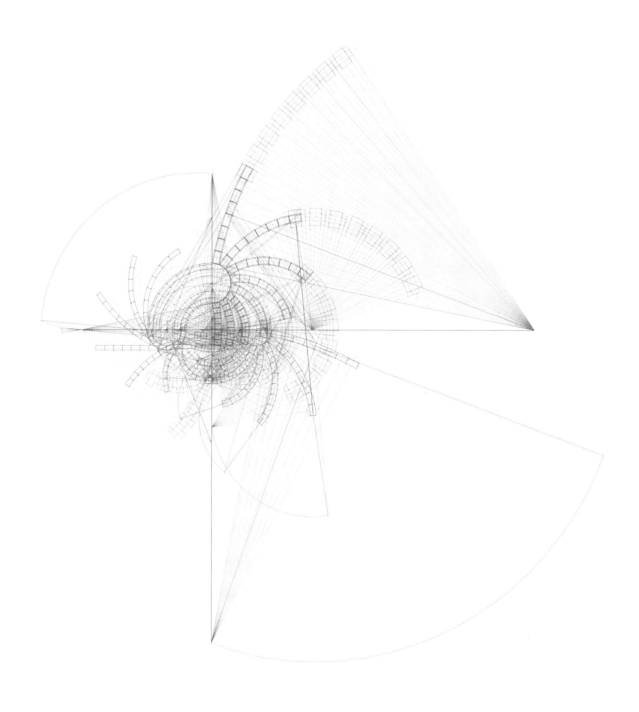

Fig 4.14
Trattato IV, Lastra XIV, Figura 8

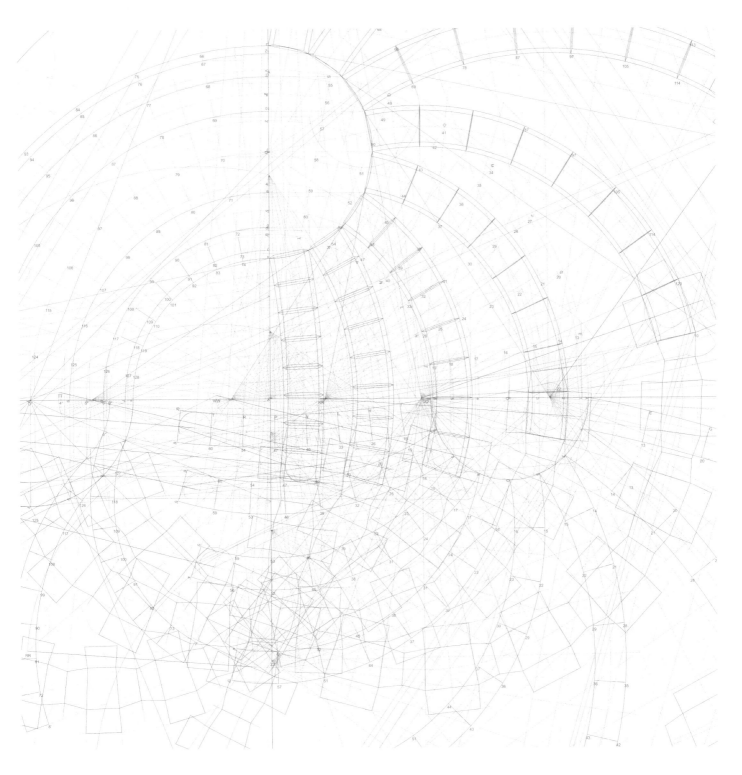

Fig 4.15
Trattato IV, Lastra XIV, Figura 8

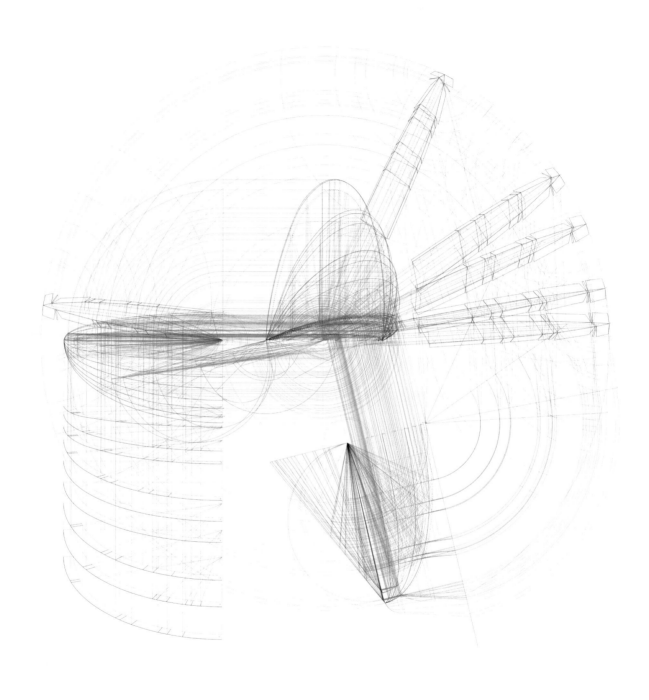

Fig 4.16
Euclid's Wedge, Asymmetric Construction

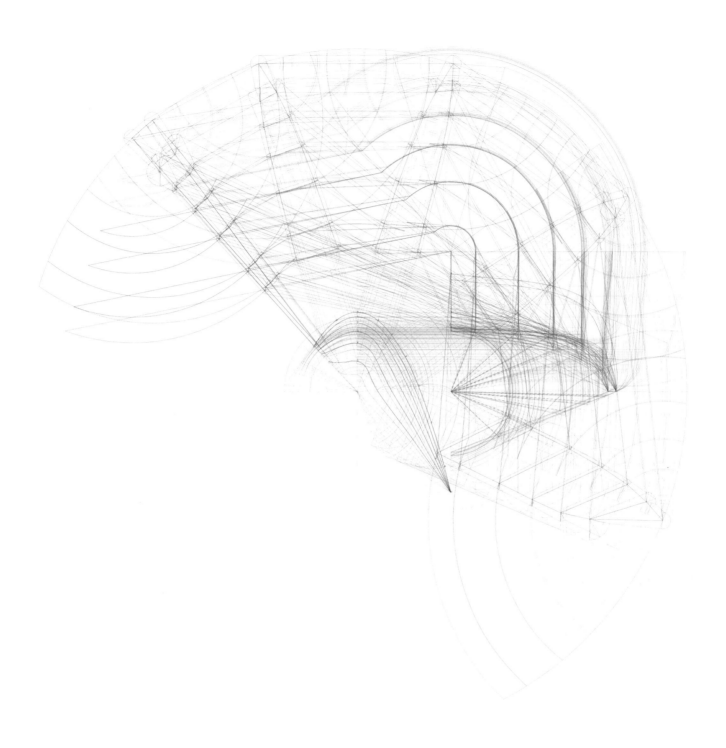

Fig 4.17
Euclid's Wedge, String Construction 01

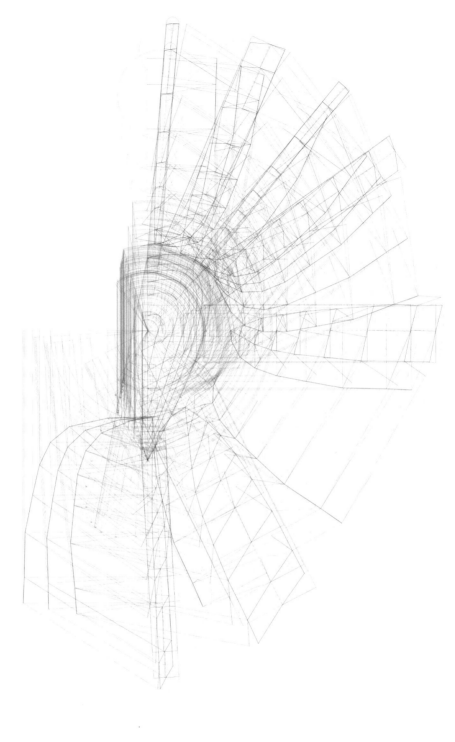

Fig 4.18
Euclid's Parabolic Wedge

Fig 4.19
Euclid's Hyperbolic Wedge

Animating Guarini[1]

In the previous sections of this book, history and formal analysis played a central role. The drawings for "Guarini Reassembled" are new, but they are bound to the historical objects that they were used to analyze. This section departs from analysis and speculates on the future potential of orthographic projection via the production of animations and their still images. The work is based on a version of orthographic projection that is no longer practiced, but it is not anchored to the past. The animations present orthographic projection and the two-dimensional surface as a thick and efficacious ground for graphic and formal inquiry, in which associations with perceptual space are fleeting. While orthographic projection is often tied to the projection of plan, section, and elevation, its underlying principles present possibilities for drawing and imaging that have little to do with seeing architecture. This departure from a reliance on visualization allows drawing to offer more while describing less—projecting uncertainty and potential with precise marks on a two-dimensional plane. What follows is a description of this departure.

Static Difference

To compute is to calculate. It is a measure of difference. Today, computation is most directly associated with digital processes. In this frame, a computation typically incorporates variable inputs and produces variable outcomes.[2] This has become one of the most basic aspects of digital processes in architecture. It is also one obvious

Opposite
Detail: Onto an Interrupted
Epicycle of Cones of Four Sides,
Elevation Oblique, Version 09

difference between seventeenth-century orthographic projection and contemporary digital practice. Guarini's drawings do not vary. He demonstrated techniques for producing templates and proportional calculations, but the examples that he provided are static. Although "Dell'ortografia gettata," title of the fourth tractate in *Architettura civile*, references movement and action through the use of the verb "*gettare*" (i.e., "to throw"), his drawings do not actually change. There is only one input and one outcome for each solution. Nevertheless, they are tied to the measurement of change.

Creating static drawings that represent change over time is a predecessor of animation, with early examples appearing in the drawings of Nicolas Oresme in the fourteenth century.[3] The first clear examples of combined orthographic projection emerged with Dürer in the early sixteenth century.[4] Durer's drawings linked two views, plan and elevation, with parallel lines to produce a combined set of projections capable of describing three-dimensional form on a two-dimensional surface.[5] Static drawings that describe change therefore precede the development of combined orthographic projection by approximately two hundred years. Furthermore, although these practices appeared at different times, they share overlapping characteristics—the first of which is the compression of multidimensional space to two dimensions, flattening time and form into legible figures on a sheet of paper. The second is that they are both contingent on the depiction of change. To understand that a figure has moved, at least two different positions must be represented. Similarly, orthographic projection requires at least two sets of information to describe a three-dimensional condition.

Guarini's "Dell'ortografia gettata" is centered on the development of templates for stonecutting, and most of the operations begin with a semicircle that then interacts with a second figure, such as a cone (FIGURE 5.1). The semicircle is thus the starting point, and its movement through space onto the cone is the transformation. The link between the starting point and its transformed state is essential both to comprehend the change and to measure it. Much like the representation of movement, the relationship between the starting point and the transformation makes the drawing more than an image. It is also a calculation of difference. While it is easy to focus on the resultant curve of the orthographic projection as the outcome of the drawing, the most important information is in the space between the initial figure and its projected transformation. A single distorted curve drawn on a flat plane cannot be more than a two-dimensional curve without its connection to a second drawing. The connection between the curves makes the drawing a graphic calculation of change

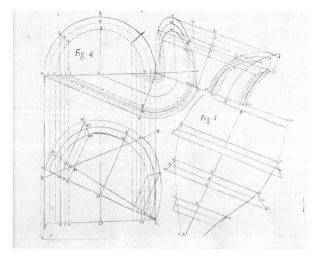

Fig 5.1

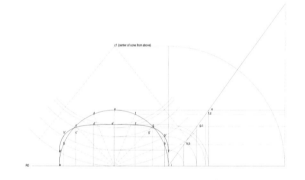

Fig 5.2

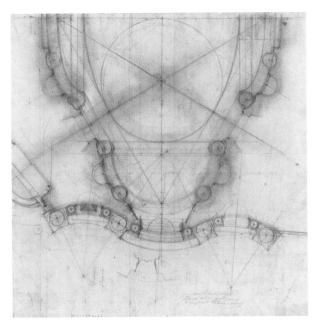

Fig 5.3

(FIGURE 5.2). Consequently, while Guarini's orthographic projections do not actually move, their intelligibility comes from the calculation of change created by drawing an object in at least two positions.

Excluding the use of orthographic projection as a form of drawing motion, animation in architecture is now a common practice. One of the early proponents of animation was Greg Lynn, in his book *Animate Form* (1999). Lynn, like many early adopters of digital technology in architecture, forcefully eschewed the disciplinary knowledge of architecture and its history in favor of direct engagement with technology: "Because of the present lack of experience and precedent with issues of motion in architecture, these issues might best be raised from within the technological regimes of the tools rather than from within architectural history."[6] In opposition to this, recent writings by Lynn have been critical of the early digital work of the 1990s because it began without a "hypothesis" or "disciplinary criteria" and was therefore compelled to repeat itself.[7] Regardless, *Animate Form* is replete with historical references and "disciplinary criteria," positioning itself not in a vacuum of technological advancement without lineage but rather in dialogue with the past. Early in *Animate Form*, Lynn discussed Baroque architecture to distinguish the formal and geometric qualities of topology from the formal characteristics of the Baroque. He began by comparing Borromini's compound curve and the calculus-based spline curve. The text that accompanies the illustration of the two types of curves describes the compound curve as composed of "fixed radii" and the spline as composed of "control vertices" through which the "spline flows."[8] Thus, Lynn argued that the compound curve is generated by the assembly of discrete static elements. In contrast, the spline curve is generated by movement and force. His point is clear: the compound curve is static and irresponsive; the spline curve is variable and responsive, and this is not a value-free comparison. It positions the development of calculus-based digital modeling as a radical break with and departure from the history of architectural drawing.

Lynn made a geometric error in this description, one that points to an alternate reading of these two curves and their materialization in drawing. Within the text describing his illustrations, Lynn referred to an earlier illustration of an "ellipse." The referenced figure is described in the captions as an "ellipse constructed with four circles with four radii."[9] This is the geometric description of an oval not an ellipse. An oval is a figure constructed of four circles to produce a closed curve that is a composite of parts of the four circles (i.e., a composite curve).[10] An ellipse is generated by a point moving about two other points whose sum of distances is fixed.[11] This means that each position of the point at the circumference of the ellipse is not at a fixed radii. It also means that the curve is not a composite but rather a singular form defined by the relationship between three points. To further complicate the issue, Borromini's plan, the source of Lynn's analysis, is an oval (FIGURE 5.3). This would seem to suggest that substituting "oval" for "ellipse" in Lynn's text would solve the problem and allow the argument to continue without error, and it would. However, the blur between Lynn's ellipse and oval opens up a line of inquiry into the materialization of geometry.

While Borromini's curve is composed of fixed points and radii, these are the material circles used to figure a more complex operation based on motion. The overall plan of Borromini's Church of San Carlo alle Quattro Fontane—the subject of Lynn's analysis—is a central oval with four large niches about its perimeter. The general form of this plan—that of a round figure with a center punctuated by a number of niches of similarly round form equally displaced about the center— exists in a number of other Baroque churches, with their precedent in the centrally planned tombs of antiquity. Furthermore, in his analysis of Guarini's unbuilt sanctuary at Oropa, historian George L. Hersey linked centrally planned architecture to the now long-defunct model of planetary movement: the epicycle (FIGURE 5.4).[12] Hersey argued that each niche in a centrally planned church is created by a point spinning about the orbit of a central radial movement.[13] The outer point defines the perimeter, while the inner radius operates as the governing geometry—binding the form to an invisible and mobile center. Centrally planned buildings and their drawings are static and in no way imply movement. However, their organization is generated by the concept of movement—a movement capable of transforming a circle into another curve that does not have fixed radii, such as an ellipse.[14] Thus, one way of seeing the Baroque compound curve is as a static composition of fixed centers, fixed radii, and tangents, but an alternate reading is that the fixed centers, radii, and tangents of the compound curve are simply the materialization of an abstract curve defined by the movement of an epicycle. In the Baroque example, the process is completed with a compass. In the contemporary spline curve, the geometry is materialized by the plotter. Both drawings, despite the underlying concepts of movement, are static.

The deposited marks of drawings on paper do not move. They reference movement and are formed by geometric abstractions of motion. While they may deploy geometry in their construction, they are also not geometry: "If we construct a material circle, measure its radius and circumference, and see if the ratio of these two lengths is equal to π, what shall we have done? We shall have made an experiment

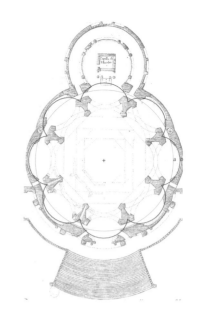

Fig 5.4

Fig 5.5

Fig 5.6

Fig 5.4
Guarino Guarini, Unbuilt Sanctuary at Oropa,
Architettura civile
The plan of Oropa can be generated by tracing point
B at a fixed radius around another point moving along
circle *A*. The resultant curve does not have a fixed radius.
The cusps are not circular segments. They are curves
generated by motion.

Fig 5.5
Detail: Onto an Interrupted Epicycle of Cones
of Four Sides, Version 14
Using lines to approximate curves is common in both
contemporary and seventeenth-century drawings. This
animation extends the drawing practice by approxi-
mating conic sections with a four-sided polygon.

Fig 5.6
Detail: Onto an Interrupted Epicycle of Tori, Version 03
Variation at the center of the animation is limited to
variation in radius. This variation then controls the
height of each subsequent projection regardless of the
receiving surface.

on the properties of the matter with which we constructed this *round thing*, and of that which the measure used was made."[15] As Poincare argued, a "material" object is distinct from its geometric definition. If the materialization of a circle produces only a "round thing," then materialization of a spline curve and an epicycle in drawing simply produces a different variety of "round things," both of which are fixed. The properties of the geometric objects are not associated with their graphic and material translations but rather with the geometric principles that govern their formation. The geometric operations that produce both the drawing of the spline curve and the drawing of the epicycle are translated into a static set of coordinates when they are materialized in ink. Borromini's plan was completed with a compass and straight edge. Lynn's spline curve was created by a computer and later by the gridded movements of the plotter.[16]

In both the epicycle and orthographic projection, movement is used in the development of architectural drawing. However, the instruments of representation impose limits on the ability of the geometric relationships to define drawings and objects. Before they could be materialized on paper or stone, they first had to be translated into formats that could be made with the tools available.[17] While texts such as *Animate Form* have been careful to distinguish the digital advances in architectural representation and fabrication from the historical lineage of architectural drawing, this argument has been based largely on the limits and differences in technology. Closer examination of orthographic projection reveals a practice that is founded on an understanding of motion and measurable difference. While these principles are not part of the disciplinary understanding of the practice, they have enormous potential to be translated into new forms of drawing and imaging.

Translation

Orthographic projection is in a tenuous position. It is currently a form of simulated mark-making on a two-dimensional medium to describe architectural form. It is only a truncated reference to a complex geometric technique that is no longer practiced. However, if it were considered a series of operations and rules used to calculate form independent of the conventions of visualization, the problem would be different. It would become a problem of translation in lieu of simulation. Rules initially used to govern the relationship of marks on a piece of paper or stone can be used to govern relationships in a digital environment, producing distinct images independent of references to historical media or no images at all.

Because Guarini's *Architettura civile* was completed by Vittone long after his death, it is unclear if the orthographic projections contained in "Dell'ortografia gettata" are Guarini's originals or Vittone's interpretations of his text. "Dell'ortografia gettata" could therefore be a translation of the procedures set out in Guarini's incomplete manuscript. The following sections describe another translation. The process began with the analysis and reconstruction of Guarini's drawings described in "Reassembling Guarini." It then shifted to translating Guarini's observations into sets of instructions (i.e., code) for the production of digital animations. All the animations are two-dimensional, and all calculation was confined to operations on a two-dimensional plane. There are no surfaces, three-dimensional objects, or three-value coordinates. The animations are two-dimensional orthographic projections of ordinary geometry (FIGURE 5.5).

Invariance

Guarini demonstrated that parallel sections through an ellipsoid vault could be generated through the use of Euclid's intercept theorem. As we have seen, the intercept theorem establishes a proportional relationship between nonparallel lines via the use of parallel projectors.[18] Guarini used this process to establish a set of intersecting lines composed of the major and minor diameter of the generating ellipse. Once parallel lines are added at intervals equivalent to a specific subdivision of the ellipse, it is a short step to deriving the true dimensions of a set of parallel sections through an ellipsoid vault. The sections vary, but because they are parallel to one another, they are proportional variations of the same invariant type, an ellipse. Guarini capitalized on this fact. He could construct all the necessary drawings of the vault from calculations deduced from a single curve, using the drawing as a calculator. He measured distances using the intercept theorem and then plotted the distances into a polar grid to obtain the resulting elliptical profile.[19] Similarly, this project constrains variation through three techniques.

The first technique is taken directly from Guarini. As we have seen, in almost all of Guarini's drawings, the semicircle is the starting point. Similarly, all the animations in this project begin with a semicircle and vary their radius over time to produce variation across the projections. This is a limited form of variation because it is confined to size alone (FIGURE 5.6).

The second form of variation has to do with the receiving sections of the projection. All the animations begin with a projection of one source curve onto the section of a specific geometric object.

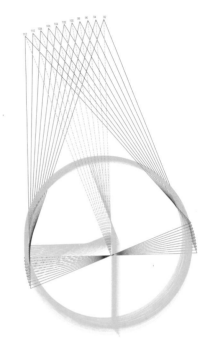

Fig 5.7

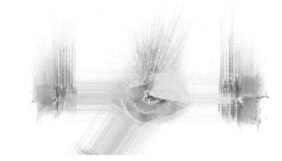

Fig 5.8

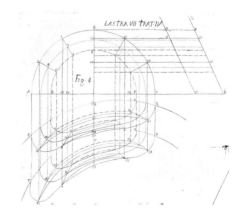

Fig 5.9

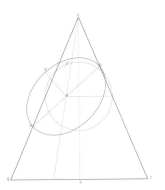

Fig 5.10

Fig 5.7
Variable Triangle as Cone
The triangle varies in its angle of orientation and the width of its base. Once this is read as the section of a cone, circular sections at the plane of intersection can be used to calculate the shape and size of the corresponding conic section by the method described in Figure 5.10.

Fig 5.8
Detail: Onto an Interrupted Epicycle of Cones from a Variable Conic Section, Version 04
This animation begins with a variable conic section as the source curve.

Fig 5.9
Guarino Guarini, *Architettura civile*,
Trattato IV, Lastra VII, Figura 4
The receiving profile of the projection (i.e., two cones) appears as two parallel lines in section and as arcs in plan.

Fig 5.10
Conic Section Measuring
To find the ellipse that corresponds to line *AB*, if triangle *QVR* is a cone:
1. Project midpoint *X* perpendicularly to line *AB*.
2. Construct a circle centered on centerline *C* at the height of point *X*.
3. Intersect the circle with the vertical projection of *X* to get *X'*.
4. Rotate *X'* about *X* until it intersects the perpendicular projection of *X* from step 1.
5. The minor diameter of the ellipse is *XX'*.
6. The major diameter of the ellipse is *AB*.

The sections have been limited to those of cones, cylinders, and tori. However, in the course of an animation, the height, width, and orientation of the sectional profile of a given figure changes. The cone oscillates and scales, changing the angle of intersection and the diameter with each new projection (FIGURE 5.7). The cylinder also scales and changes position, and the toroidal section changes from an ellipse of such a small minor diameter that it approaches a line, through a circle, and onto a horizontally attenuated ellipse.

The last form of variation introduces a variable conic section as the source curve for all the projections. A vertical line intersects an oscillating triangle, producing measurements that are used to orthographically construct the corresponding conic sections. While the variable conic section, the source curve for all the subsequent projections, changes between circle, ellipse, parabola, and hyperbola, the curvature is consistently bound to the limits of a conic section, producing variation on an invariant type. This continuity allows the animation to produce a large set of variable curves that remain measurable through their link with a known source figure (FIGURE 5.8).

Minimal Figures

Guarini's drawings represent each geometric object with as little information needed to describe its form. An example of this can be found in the fifteenth observation of chapter three in the fourth tractate (FIGURE 5.9).[20] In this case, two cones were drawn with two parallel lines in the upper right-hand corner of the drawing, and two arcs in the lower left. This reduces the description of the cones to their most basic geometric properties: height, radius, and center.

Similarly, within the animations of this project, cones are represented as triangles in section, and their dimensional properties are extracted through a measuring algorithm that follows the same logic that Guarini used. The major diameter of an elliptical conic section can be found by measuring the total length of the line passing through both sides of a given triangle. The minor diameter can be found by projecting the midpoint of the previous line perpendicularly until it intersects a circle centered on the cone at the same height as the midpoint (FIGURE 5.10). The operation and the subsequent algorithm eliminate the need to represent whole objects through constructed "views." Instead, the properties of the object are used to find the required measurements without any additional graphic information. This allows the animations to calculate a large number of curves without resorting to the representation of fixed perceptual space. The curves are animated in a state of perpetual change (FIGURE 5.11).

Primitive Templates

The cone, sphere, and cylinder are geometric solids derived from a circle. Within a digital framework, a cone is a singular object (i.e., a primitive), a built-in component in most software platforms. The same can be said for the sphere or the cylinder. However, these singular forms are composed of sets of simpler geometric elements: the circle, the line, and the point. In the history of architectural drawing, the ability to break down the cone, sphere, and cylinder into specific geometric properties has made these figures not only significant formal elements but also drawing instruments in their own right. Guarini used cones to unroll toroidal vaults, hemispherical domes, and systematically distorted semicircles. The three simple solids can therefore be understood as geometric elements capable of describing forms of a higher degree of complexity than themselves. By extending this logic into the digital realm, it is possible to imagine geometric primitives as two-dimensional drawing instruments capable of describing form through flat, two-dimensional orthographic projections.

Fig 5.11

In the ninth observation of chapter three in the fourth tractate, Guarini provided a method of projecting a semicircle onto a cylinder.[21] Referencing Euclid, he bypassed a large amount of projection by providing a template as a drawing device. The drawing device is the section through the cylinder at the angle of intersection. This template is so specific that it can be used for no other task.[22]

The same principle is used in this project. All the dimensions extracted from the "minimal figures" in section are then fed into the production of templates in plan that vary in shape and size (FIGURE 5.12A–D). All the templates, regardless of whether they comprise curved or linear elements (polygons), vary between the bounding figure of either an ellipse or a circle. Whereas Guarini produced a single template, the animations use a series of variable templates at each instance of intersection (FIGURE 5.13).

Fig 5.12

Interrupted Epicycles

Guarini's drawings do not move and do not vary over time. However, the end of his treatise contains the drawings of his centrally planned churches. The figure of a centrally planned church can be linked to the kinematic figures of epicycloids and hypocycloids.[23] Epicycloids and hypocycloids are produced by the orbit of one point rotating about another point that is rotating about a fixed center. An epicycloid produces convex curvature, while a hypocycloid produces concave curvature. If one imagines that the centrally planned churches at

Fig 5.12a

Fig 5.12b

Fig 5.12c

Fig 5.12d

Fig 5.12e

Fig 5.11
Detail: Onto an Interrupted Epicycle of Cones, Version 18
At the upper right-hand corner of the image, the vertices of all the triangles used to generate the conic sections are numbered. The measuring process appears as a gray blur of circles at the base of the triangles.

Fig 5.12
Process of Measurement and Projection
Diagrams a–e explain the process of orthographically projecting a semicircle onto a single eccentric epicycle of tori:
a. Projection of the semicircle onto a variable section of a torus
b. Measurement of the intersection
c. Translation of the measurements into circles and ellipses on an epicycle
d. Horizontal projection onto the epicycle
e. Plotting of curves with a polyline

the end Guarini's treatise are generated by continuously rotating objects, the path of rotation is fixed. The epicycloid or hypocycloid that generates one centrally planned figure continues to generate that figure infinitely without variation (FIGURES 5.14, 5.15). While the figure is created by movement, it is an intentionally limited movement. The final revolution is the same as its starting revolution.

The animated drawings of this project are created with a procedure to generate variation over time. The motion of the epicycloid is no longer limited to completing a fixed number of rotations about a given cycle. Instead, the number of rotations changes (FIGURES 5.16A, B; 5.17A, B). The epicycloid is interrupted, shifting simultaneously from a cycle of four rotations per revolution to eight or one hundred (FIGURE 5.18). Furthermore, because all regular polygons can be derived from a circle, each incidence of rotation shifts between varying degrees of curve approximation. The epicycloid, instead of being a fixed entity, transforms into a movement that describes figures oscillating between the curvilinear and the polygonal, the multiple and the singular. All the animations move along the path of an interrupted epicycle. The orthographic projection, instead of being a fixed and known quantity, shifts and follows the path of a constantly changing set of oscillating points (FIGURE 5.19).

Fig 5.13

Reversible Projections

Two-dimensional orthographic projection operates by describing any object with two sets of information in which all the objects' measurements are taken into account. This does not mean that each set of information must correspond to a visual representation of the entire object; it must only provide all metric information necessary to describe that object.[24] Several scholars have noted the use of the semicircle as central in stereotomy not only for structural reasons but also for reasons of reversibility.[25] Because Guarini began with the semicircle in almost all of the examples in "Dell'ortografia gettata," this allowed him to work in reverse toward the original planar figure of the semicircle when solving problems of measurement. A key example of this is a barrel vault generated by projecting a semicircle onto a cone. In this instance, Guarini unrolled the original semicircle to obtain the unrolled dimensions of the complex curves of intersection. Because the semicircle is connected to the distorted circle with parallel lines, unrolling the original semicircle results in unrolling the more complex distorted curve.[26]

Reversibility is only useful if the starting point is simpler than the result. It creates a direct link between a known and measurable

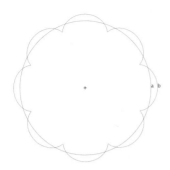

Fig 5.14

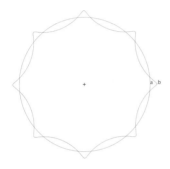

Fig 5.15

Fig 5.13
Onto an Interrupted Epicycle of Tori, Version 10
This toroidal projection includes elevations that
have been projected radially around 180 degrees of
the epicycle.

Fig 5.14
An epicycle of six cusps at one revolution.

Fig 5.15
A hypocycle of six cusps at one revolution.

source figure with an unknown and nameless curve. It was practical for Guarini and allowed him to explore a wide range of forms while maintaining the conceptual link to a predictable geometric figure: the circle.

This same process is built into the animations. Each projection is unrolled from its elevation by cross-referencing the heights of the original semicircle or conic section with the horizontal information in the elevations. The dimensions of the original semicircle are unrolled upon a line in conjunction with all the irregular curves generated by a given instance of projection (FIGURE 5.20).

Dead Geometry

Architect Jane Burry has argued that orthographic projection is "on its way to join the reliable ranks of dead and dormant geometries."[27] For Burry, this denotes orthographic projection's future obsolescence in the face of digital computation. She argued that other modes of representation are emerging that are not based on links to perceptual space and that these modes will have more relevance in the development of future architecture.

The phrase "dead and dormant geometries" is a reference to Evan's description of orthographic projection. Evans argued that a dead geometry is a geometry whose fundamental tenants are no longer the subject of debate. They have been proven beyond doubt and are therefore more useful to the architect because they are an "inoculation against uncertainty."[28] As a dead geometry, orthographic projection enables architects and stonemasons to both generate and measure complex three-dimensional forms with two-dimensional drawings. Furthermore, the fact that it is dead, removing uncertainty from its operations, allows it to be reconfigured and adapted to solve idiosyncratic formal problems, making orthographic projection an enormously powerful tool in the production of architectural form. These dead geometries also give orthographic projection such enormous potential to be reimagined.

The animations presented in this chapter translate Guarini's techniques. Technology and history are intermingled to produce a set of animations and images that are two-dimensional orthographic projections but have little in common with the disciplinary convention. Although the techniques are orthographic projections, they do not describe clear architectural forms. Instead, they attempt to expose the geometric knowledge and imaginative potential that lies dormant in the disciplinary convention of orthographic drawing. Implicit in this is a proposal and argument for future relationships

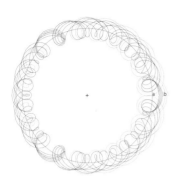

Fig 5.16a

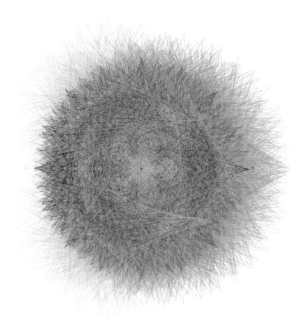

Fig 5.16b

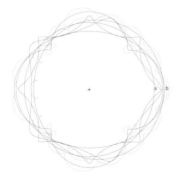

Fig 5.17a

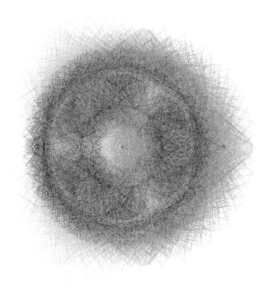

Fig 5.17b

Fig 5.18

Fig 5.20

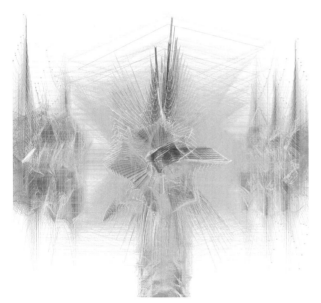

Fig 5.19

Fig 5.16a
An interrupted epicycle of six cusps at five revolutions.

Fig 5.16b
An interrupted epicycle of six cusps at fifty revolutions.

Fig 5.17a
An interrupted hypocycle of six cusps at five revolutions.

Fig 5.17b
An interrupted hypocycle of six cusps at fifty revolutions.

Fig 5.18
Detail: Onto an Interrupted Epicycle of Tori , Version 09
The direction of each projection is dictated by three points following the path
of three variable and interrelated epicycles.

Fig 5.19
Onto an Interrupted Epicycle of Cones , Version 08
This animation uses conic sections positioned in top view to plot regular
polygons. In this specific image, a four-sided polygon is used. Geometric
approximation is used generatively.

Fig 5.20
Onto an Interrupted Epicycle of Cylinders, Version 08
The leftmost portion of the image contains an oblique elevation of one
epicycle and the unrolled surface of every projected vault in the animation.
Each projection is related back to the original source figure to be unrolled. The
principle of reversibility was used in the design of the animated drawing.

between history and technology. As we continue to develop and adopt new technologies to control, generate, and image the physical world, what role can dead and dormant techniques, ideas, and geometries play? One answer has already been provided, and it seems largely inadequate: historical practices can be simulated in the manner of orthographic drawings. Another option is that history and technology can be combined to produce forms of imaging that are distinct from both. This work pursued the latter through the production of animated two-dimensional orthographic projections (FIGURE 5.21).

Fig 5.21

Fig 5.21
Onto an Interrupted Epicycle of Cones from a
Variable Conic Section, Version 01
A oscillating cone (a triangle in the animation) is cut by a plane
(a line) and then projected onto an epicycle of cones.

1   Portions of this research were presented as the paper, "Ordinary Geometry," at *Black Box: 107th ACSA Annual Conference* (Pittburgh, 2019).

2   For a general introduction, see, e.g., William Mitchell, "Introduction: A New Agenda for Computer-Aided Design," in *In the Electronic Design Studio: Architectural Knowledge and Media in the Computer Era*, ed. Malcolm McCullough, William Mitchell, and P. Purcell (Cambridge, MA: MIT Press, 1990), 1–6.

3   Sigfried Giedion, *Mechanization Takes Command: A Contribution to Anonymous History* (New York: Oxford University Press, 1948).

4   Lefèvre, "Emergence of Combined Orthographic Projection," 226.

5   See multiple images in Dürer, *Painter's Manual*.

6   Lynn, *Animate Form*, 17–18.

7   Lynn, ed., *Archaeology of the Digital*, 11.

8   Lynn, *Animate Form*, 21.

9   Ibid., 17.

10 For a clear definition on drawing an oval, see Sebastiano Serlio, *Sebastiano Serlio on Architecture*, trans. Vaughan Hart and Peter Hicks (New Haven, CT: Yale University Press, 1996).

11 D. Hilbert and S. Cohn-Vossen, *Geometry and the Imagination* (New York: Chelsea, 1952), 3.

12 George L. Hersey, *Architecture and Geometry in the Age of the Baroque* (Chicago: University of Chicago Press, 2000), 188.

13 Cameron Wu has expanded Hersey's argument by geometrically describing this kinematic process. See Cameron Wu, "Of Circles and Lines," *Log*, no. 31 (Spring/Summer 2014): 107–14.

14 Hilbert and Cohn-Vossen, *Geometry and the Imagination*, 277–80.

15 Henri Poincare, *Science and Hypothesis* (New York: Science Press, 1913), 82; emphasis original.

16 Except for the case of the pen plotter, most printers convert vector-based drawings to raster-based images before printings. See Casey Reas and Ben Fry, *Processing: A Programming Handbook for Visual Designers and Artists* (Cambridge, MA: MIT Press, 2007), 603–12.

17 There were several tools available to draw noncircular curves during the Baroque era. However, at the scale of a building, the geometry still needed to be translated into something the mason could draw on site. For a detailed discussion of such drawing devices, see Andrew Witt, "Machine Epistemology in Architecture," trans. Annette Wiethuchter, *Candide: Journal for Architectural Knowledge*, no. 3 (December 2010): 37–88.

18 Field and Gray, *Geometrical Work of Girard Desargues*, 5.

19 See the chapter "Reassembling Guarini" for a more detailed explanation of this process.

20 For further explanation of the representation of cones, see the chapter "On Redrawing."

21 Guarini, *Architettura civile*.

22 See the section "Strong Card" in the chapter "Reassembling Guarini" for a more detailed analysis of Guarini's original drawings. For the original text See Guarini, *Architettura civile*, 206–7.

23 Hersey, *Architecture and Geometry*, 186–189.

24 A cylinder can be represented by a rectangle and circle, and from this information, every point on the surface of the cylinder can be found.

25 See, e.g., Robin Evans, "Translations from Drawing to Buildings," in *Translations from Drawing to Building and Other Essays* (Cambridge, MA: MIT Press, 1997), 153–89.

26 See the section "Reversibility" in the chapter "Reassembling Guarini" for more on this.

27 Jane Burry, "The Shifting Ground of Architectural Geometry: Getting to Know the New Representational Space," in "Geometry and Architecture," ed. Stephen Frith, special issue, *Architectural Theory Review* 15, no. 2 (August 2010): 187–200, 188.

28 Evans, *Projective Cast*, xxvi – xxvii.

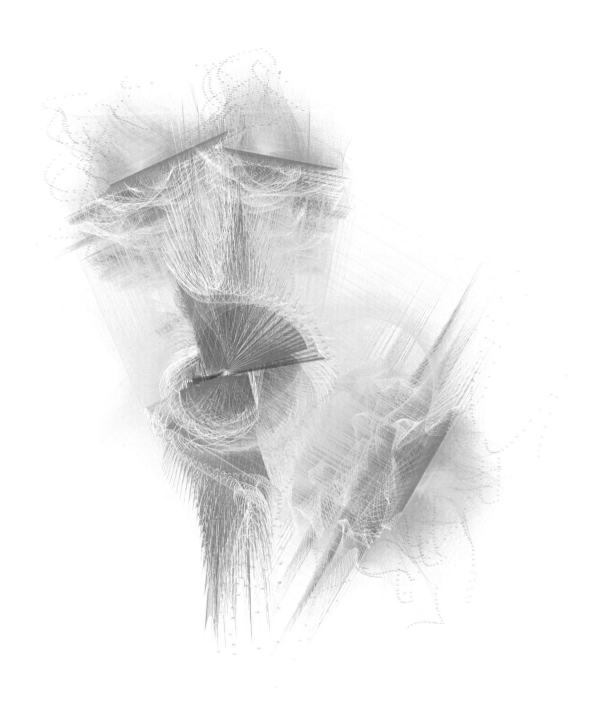

Fig 6.1
Onto an Interrupted Epicycle of Cones, Elevation Oblique, Version 05b

Guarini Animated

COLLECTION OF THIRTY DRAWINGS

The images in this chapter, as in all other chapters of the book, are two-dimensional orthographic projections. However, unlike the drawings in "Guarini Reassembled" they are stills from an animation. The process involves translating Guarini's operations into the high-level (i.e., easy-to-understand) programming language of Python. Each operation (e.g., the intersection of two lines or the measurement of a conic section from a triangle) is translated into a function that provides a list of numeric values. These values are then used to generate graphic representations in the open-source programming environment of Processing. In the early animations, two graphic representations were used: the line and the ellipse. In the later iterations, everything was created using only lines. All the geometric operations were limited to calculations based on two-value coordinates, thereby confining all drawing to a two-dimensional plane—the intent of which was both to maintain a proximity to the geometry of the source and to focus all the work on the development of two-dimensional form.

The animations use a single color expressed in values of red, green, and blue, which are scaled across different lines within the drawing until they approach the value corresponding to white.[1] Line weight corresponds to the conventions of descriptive geometry, in which object lines are thicker and construction lines are thinner. All lines are solid.

Each animation is generated by the movement of three different points about three interrelated epicycloids or hypocycloids. All text within the animations corresponds to labeling the three epicycloids as "a," "b," or "c." When an animation contains three distinct projections, each projection corresponds to an elevation oblique to one of the epicycloids or hypocycloids. When the projections overlap continuously into a round field, each elevation has been projected perpendicularly to a plan at a given instance of projection.

All animation titles begin with, "The Two-Dimensional Orthographic Projection of a Semicircle," and end with a description of the operation on each page: "Onto an Interrupted Epicycle of...." All titles are descriptions, and all animations are two-dimensional orthographic projections.

---

1 The animations were conceived in a digital environment using an RGB color profile. The printing of this book was done in two colors: black and Pantone 292 C. The description therefore corresponds to the process of making the animations and not to the printed image.

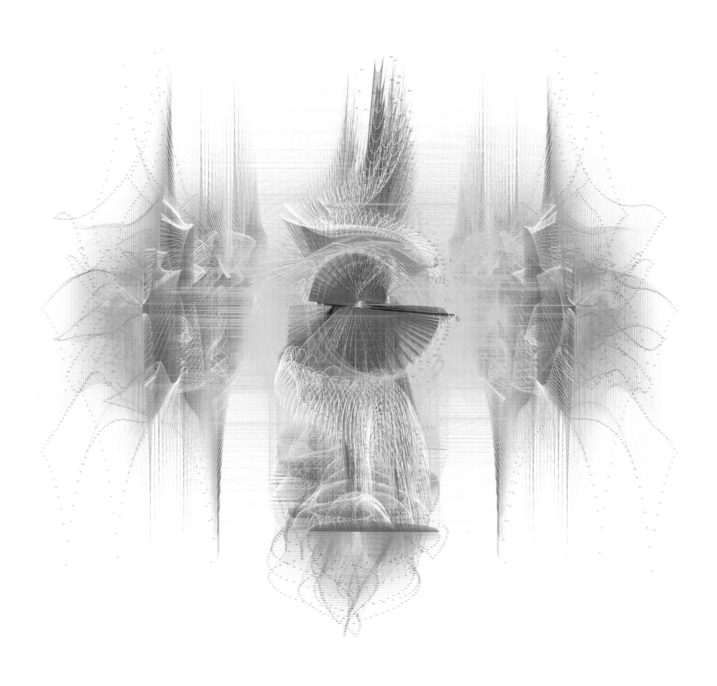

Fig 6.2
Onto an Interrupted Epicycle of Cones, Elevation Oblique, Version 05

Detail of Opposite

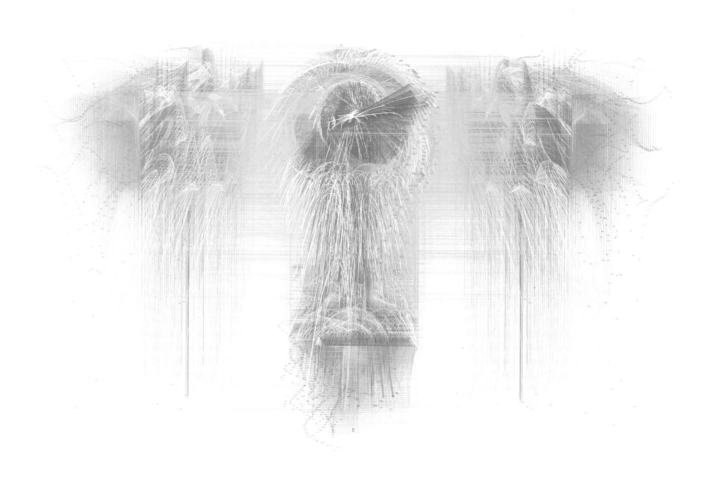

Fig 6.3
Onto an Interrupted Epicycle of Cones, Elevation Oblique, Version 01

Detail of Opposite

Fig 6.4
Onto an Interrupted Epicycle of Cones, Elevation Oblique, Version 08

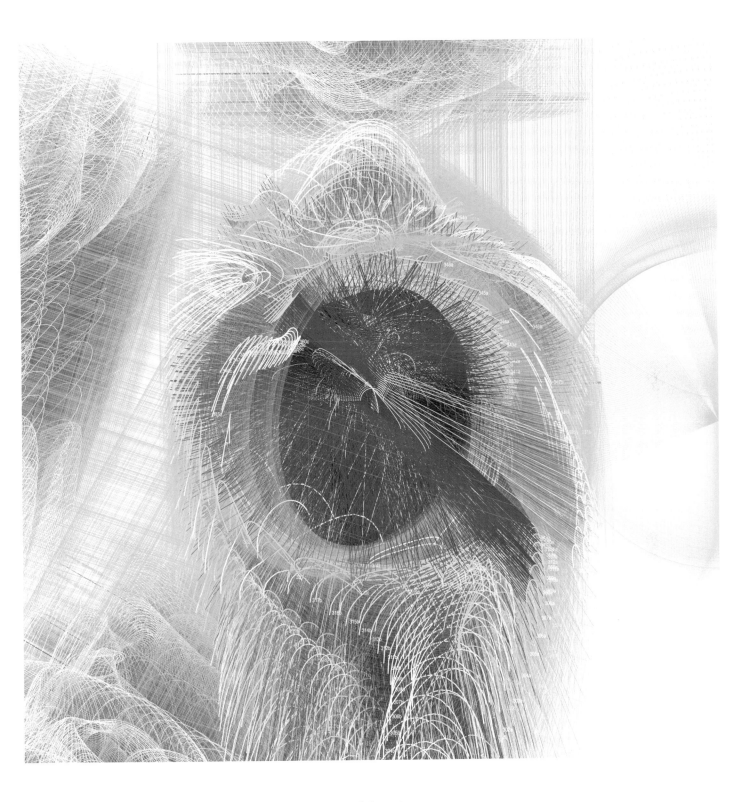

Detail of Opposite

Fig 6.5
Onto an Interrupted Epicycle of Cones, Elevation Oblique, Version 06

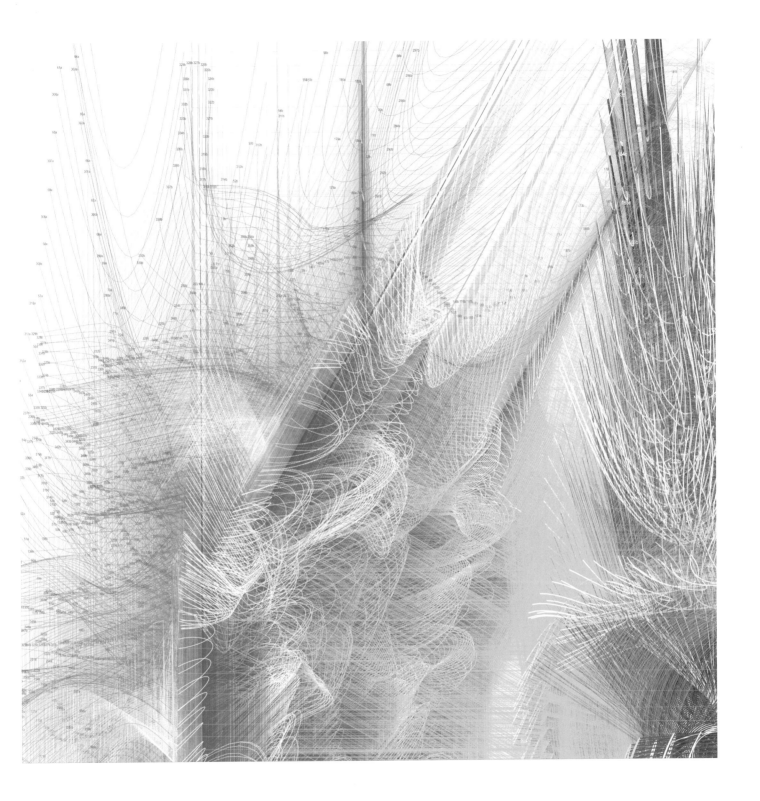

Detail of Opposite

Fig 6.6
Onto an Interrupted Epicycle of Cones, Elevation Oblique, Version 07

Detail of Opposite

Fig 6.7
Onto an Interrupted Epicycle of Cones, Radial Projection, Version 12

Detail of Opposite

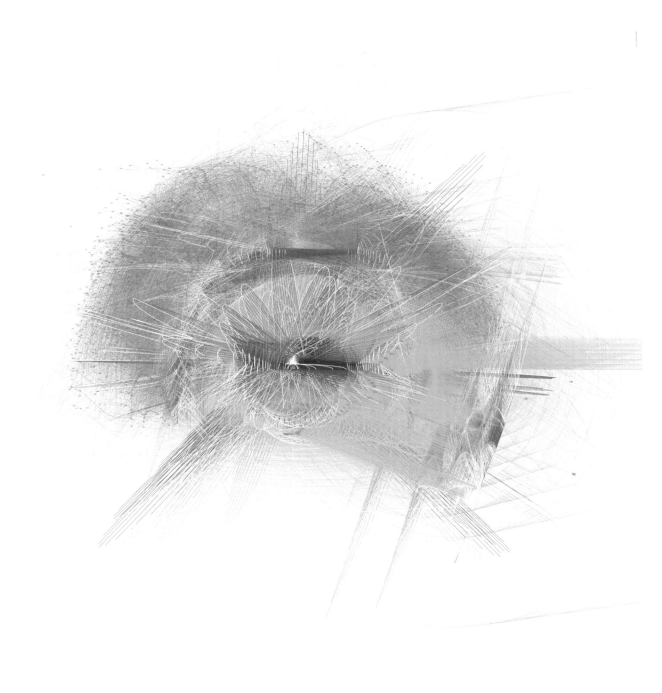

Fig 6.8
Onto an Interrupted Epicycle of Cylinders, Radial Projection, Version 13

Detail of Opposite

Fig 6.9
Onto an Interrupted Epicycle of Cylinders, Elevation Oblique, Version 14

Detail of Opposite

Fig 6.10
Onto an Interrupted Epicycle of Cones of Four Sides, Elevation Oblique, Version 14

Detail of Opposite

Fig 6.11
Onto an Interrupted Epicycle of Cones of Four Sides, Elevation Oblique, Version 21

Detail of Opposite

Fig 6.12
Onto an Interrupted Epicycle of Cones of Four Sides, Elevation Oblique, Version 08

Detail of Opposite

Fig 6.13
Onto an Interrupted Epicycle of Cones of Four Sides, Elevation Oblique, Version 22

Detail of Opposite

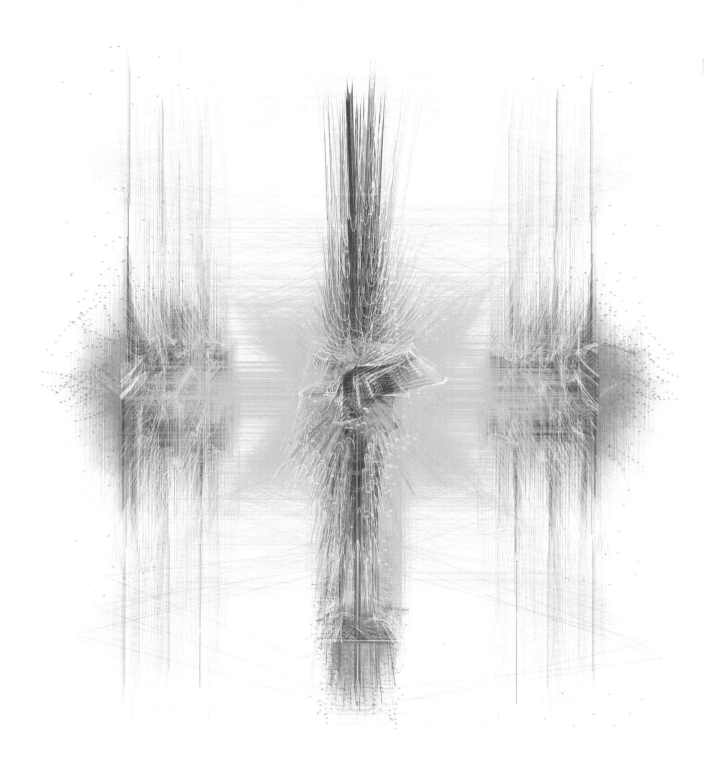

Fig 6.14
Onto an Interrupted Epicycle of Cones of Four Sides, Elevation Oblique, Version 07

Detail of Opposite

Fig 6.15
Onto an Interrupted Epicycle of Cones of Four Sides, Elevation Oblique, Version 09

Detail of Opposite

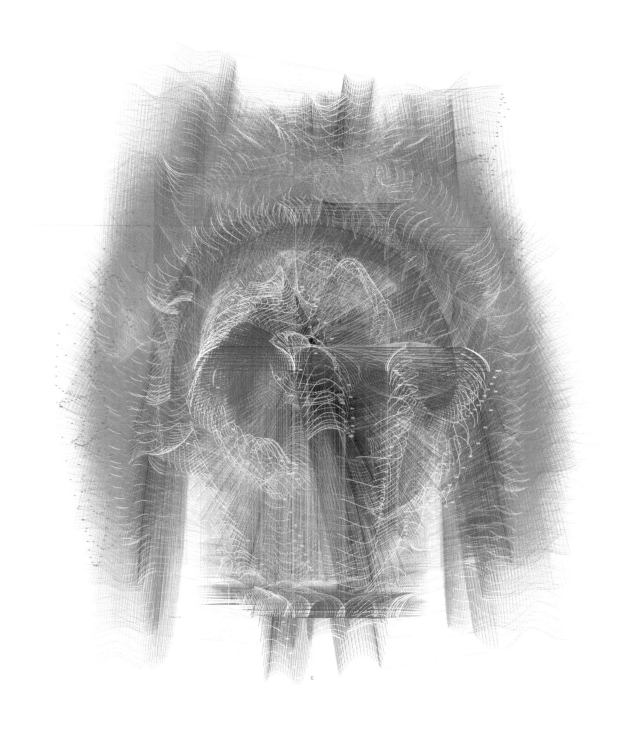

Fig 6.16
Onto an Interrupted Epicycle of Tori, Radial Projection, Version 09a

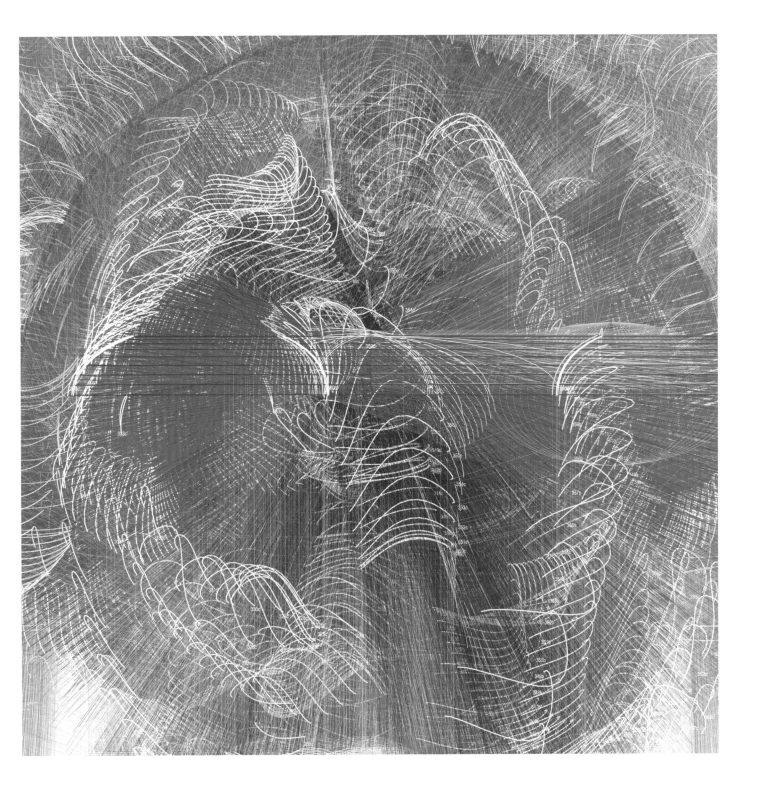

Detail of Opposite

Fig 6.17
Onto an Interrupted Epicycle of Tori, Elevation Oblique, Version 08

Detail of Opposite

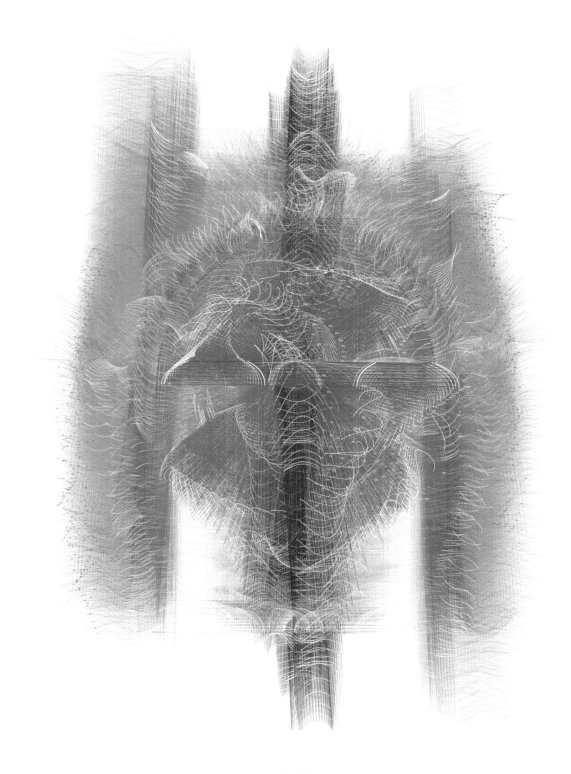

Fig 6.18
Onto an Interrupted Epicycle of Tori, Radial Projection, Version 08

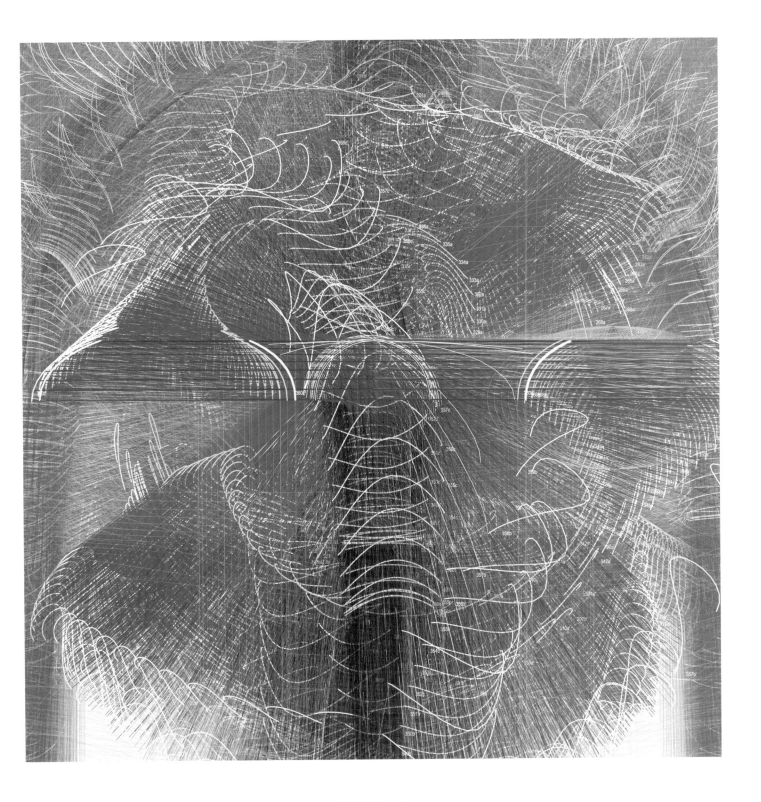

Detail of Opposite

Fig 6.19
Onto an Interrupted Epicycle of Tori, Radial Projection, Version 09b

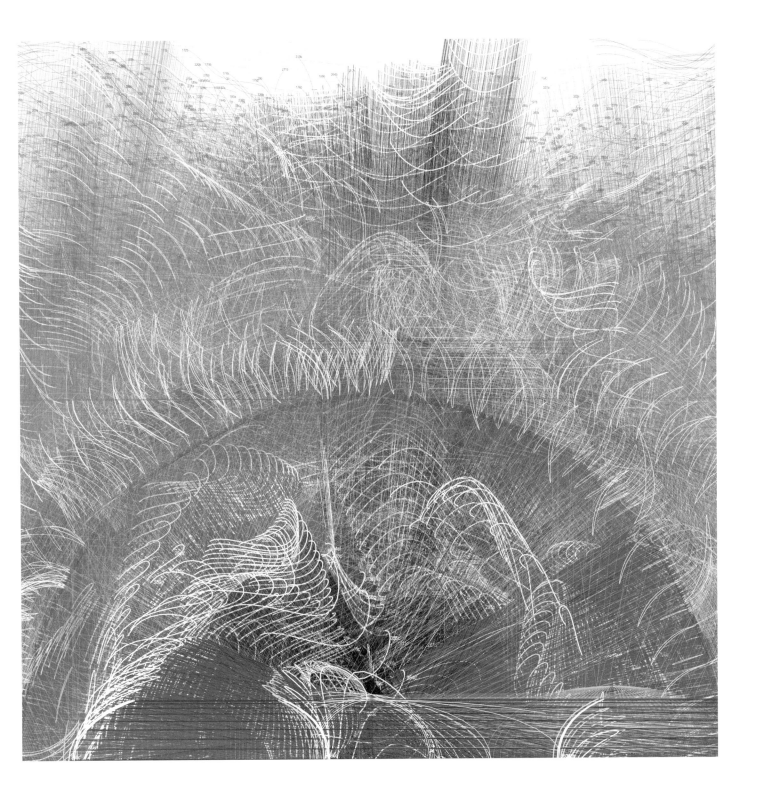

Detail of Opposite

Fig 6.20
Onto an Interrupted Epicycle of Tori, Elevation Oblique, Version 13

Detail of Opposite

Fig 6.21
Onto an Interrupted Epicycle of Tori, Elevation Oblique, Version 14

Detail of Opposite

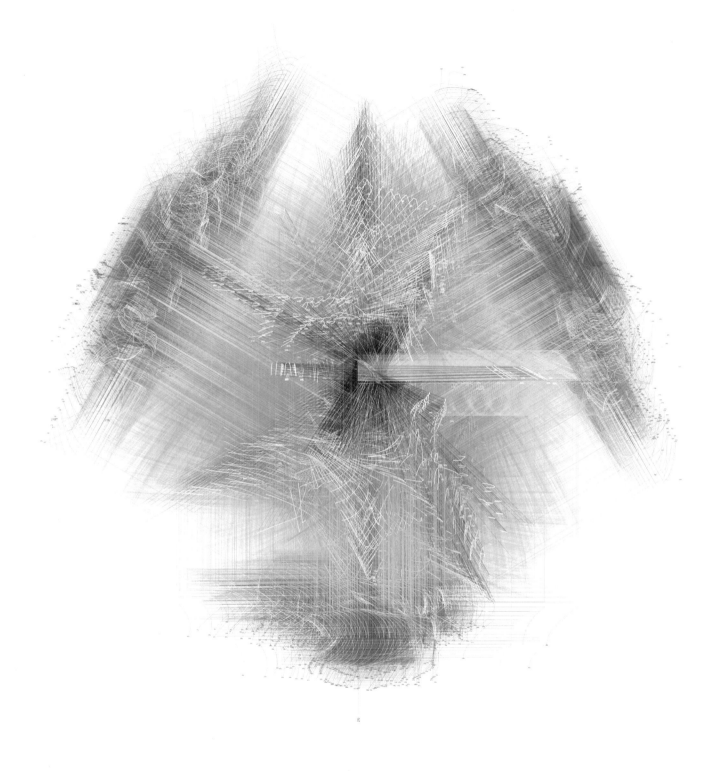

Fig 6.22
Onto an Interrupted Epicycle of Tori of Three Sides, Elevation Oblique, Version 27

Detail of Opposite

Fig 6.23
Onto an Interrupted Epicycle of Tori of Three Sides, Radial Projection, Version 15

Detail of Opposite

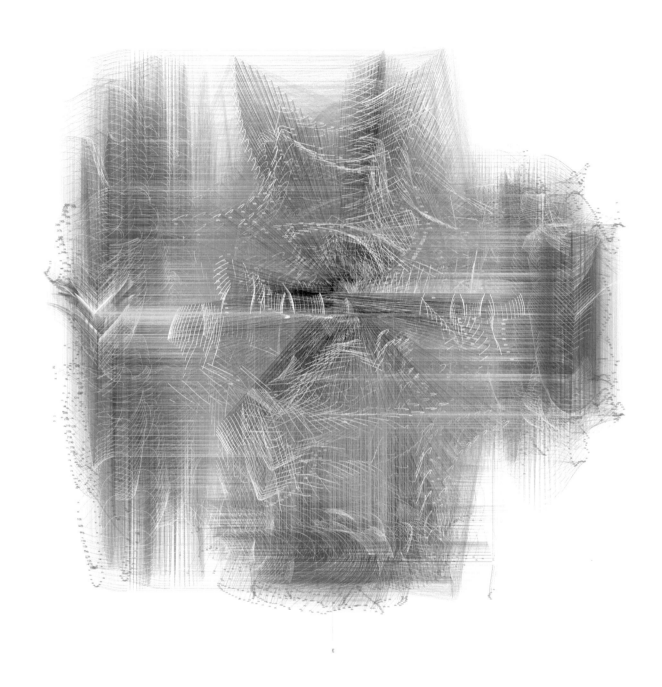

Fig 6.24
Onto an Interrupted Epicycle of Tori of Three Sides, Elevation Oblique, Version 18

Detail of Opposite

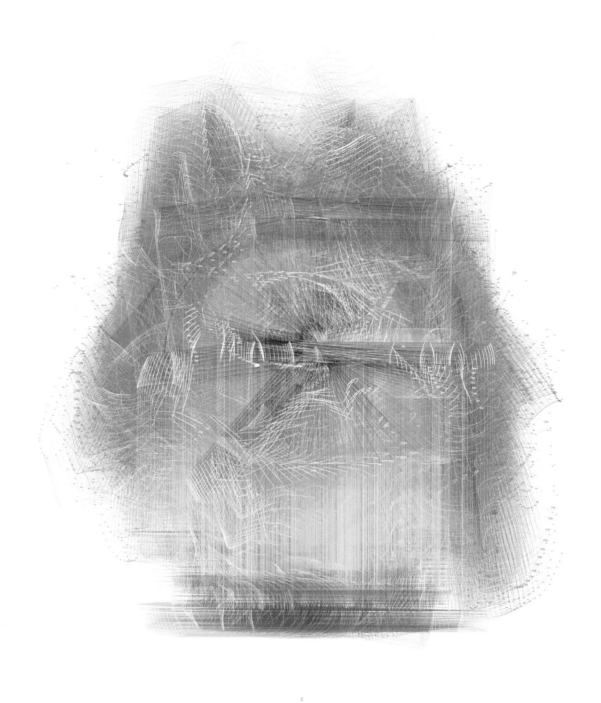

Fig 6.25
Onto an Interrupted Epicycle of Tori of Three Sides, Radial Projection, Version 18

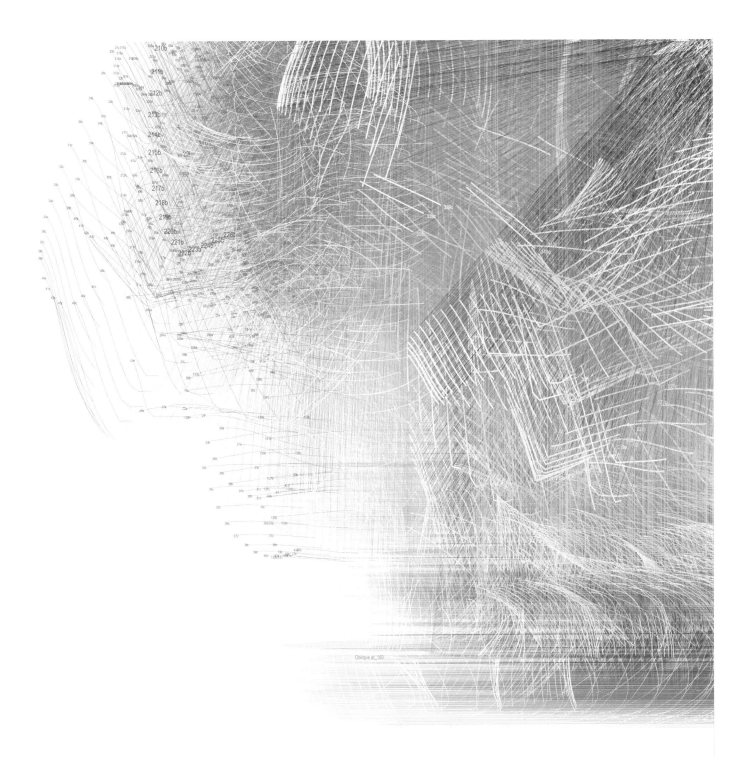

Detail of Opposite

Fig 6.26
Onto an Interrupted Epicycle of Tori of Three Sides, Elevation Oblique, Version 21

Detail of Opposite

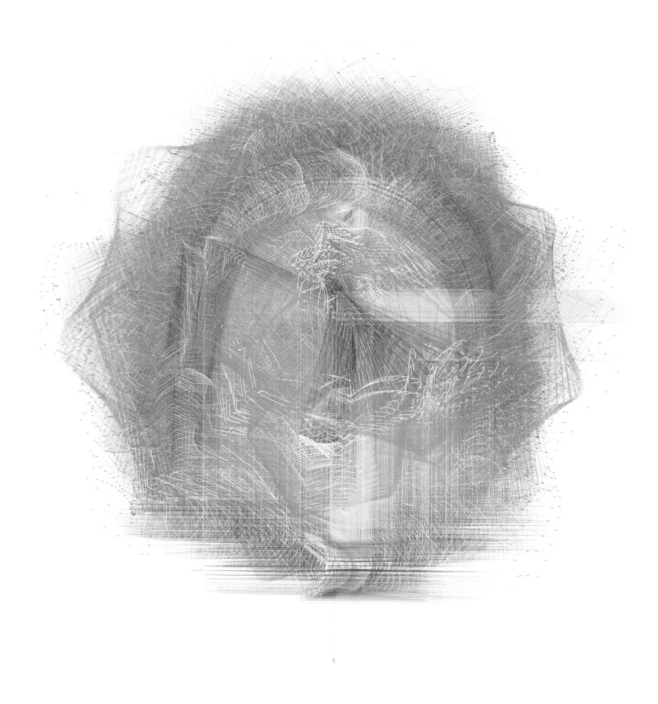

Fig 6.27
Onto an Interrupted Epicycle of Tori of Five Sides, Radial Projection, Version 14

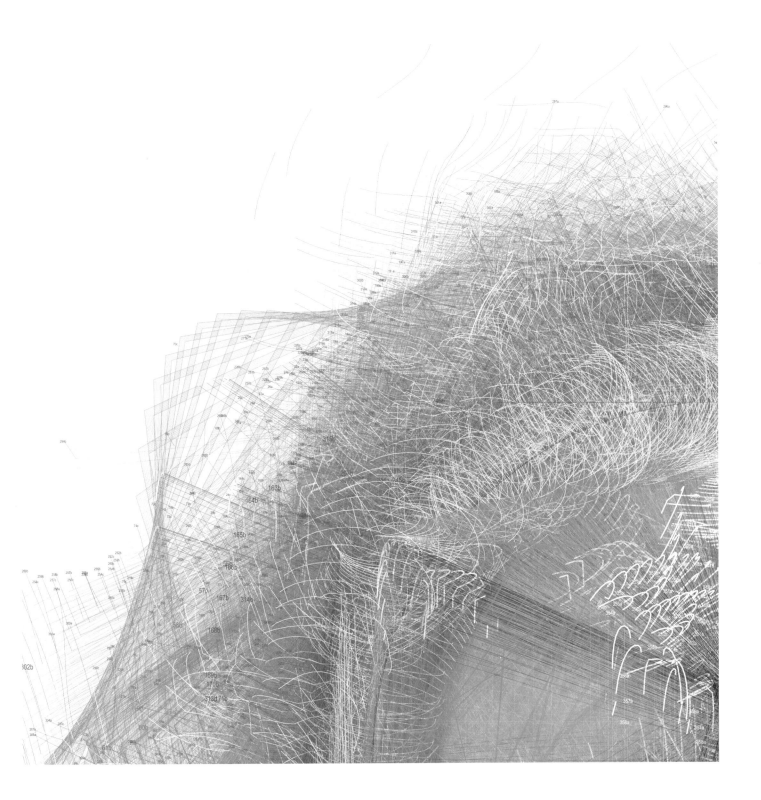

Detail of Opposite

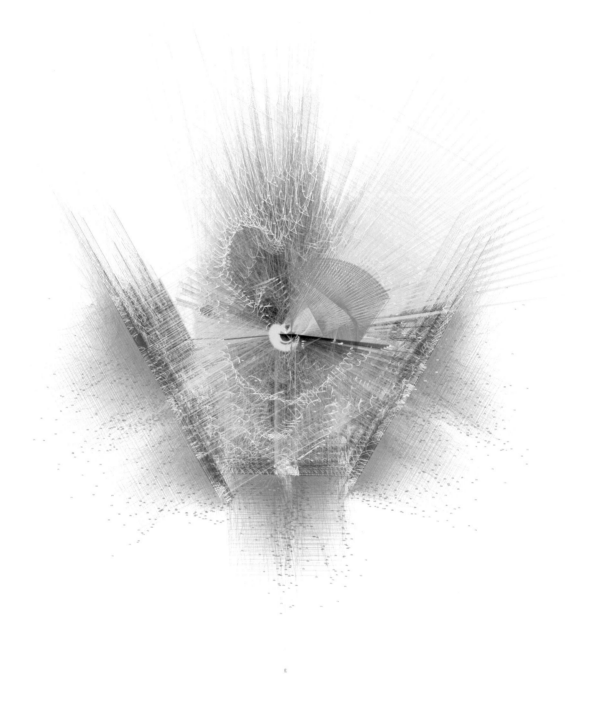

Fig 6.28
Onto an Interrupted Epicycle of Cones of Three Sides from a Variable Conic Section,
Elevation Oblique, Version 12

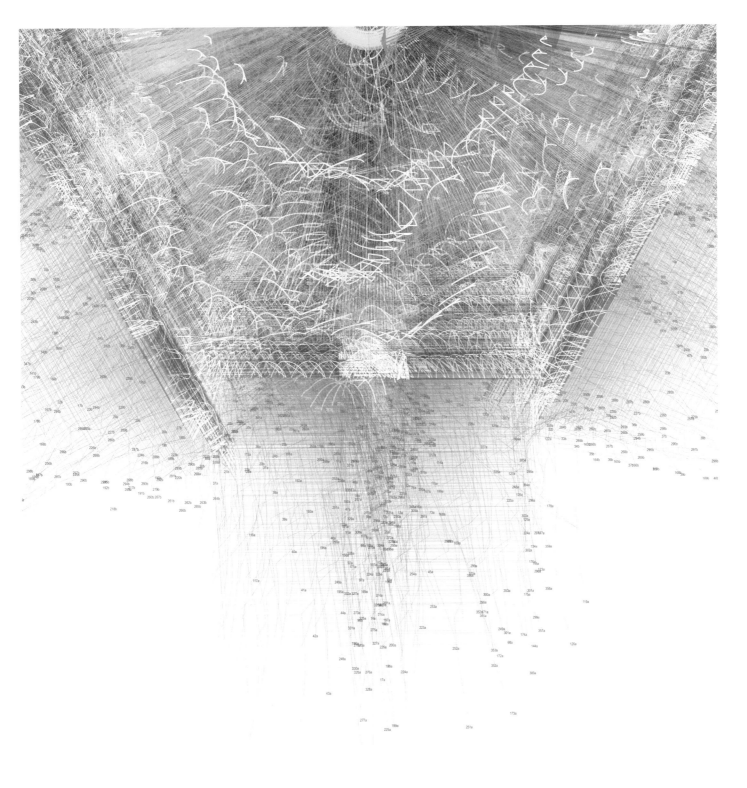

Detail of Opposite

Fig 6.29
Onto an Interrupted Epicycle of Cones of Three Sides from a Variable Conic Section,
Elevation Oblique, Version 08

Detail of Opposite

Fig 6.30
Onto an Interrupted Epicycle of Cones of Three Sides from a Variable Conic Section,
Elevation Oblique, Version 01b

Detail of Opposite

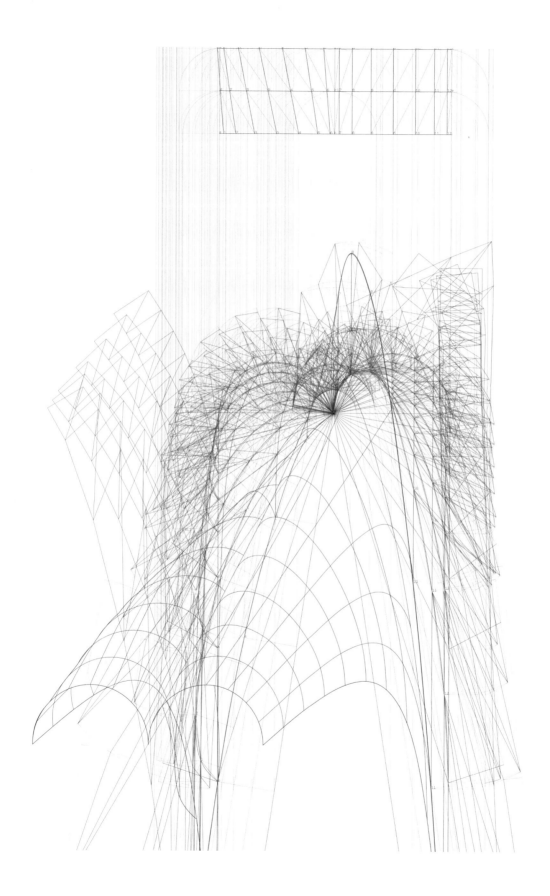

130

Guarini Explained

AN APPENDIX

One of the most compelling aspects of Guarini's "Dell'ortografia gettata" is its incompleteness. Some drawings appear to be only partially drawn, and others include differences of measurement and description between the text and the drawings. Still others leave gaps in the explanation, providing the reader with only a series of steps to follow and with little geometric justification as to why the steps should work. The gaps in the explanation and the inconsistencies leave the text and drawings open to interpretation. In this book, I have leveraged such an interpretation—working between the text and drawings to reassemble various fragments of Guarini's observations into single drawings connected by parallel lines. It is not possible to know if the reconstructions of Guarini's methods are correct, any more than it is to know which drawings are Guarini's and which are Vittone's.

The following section is a technical appendix to the drawings and text presented in this book. It explains the drawing practices deployed in the reassembly of Guarini's drawings without any attempt to correct errors in Guarini's originals. Instead, Guarini's drawings are taken as examples of a drawing practice before it became a convention—replete with the idiosyncrasies of a malleable tradition.

The chapter is composed of two types of examples. The first is the complete explanation of specific drawings from "Dell'ortografia gettata." These examples are titled in the same manner as the drawings in "Guarini Reassembled," with the exception that each title ends with word "Explained." Thus, the title "Trattato IV, Lastra VIII, Figure 4–6 Explained" is the full explanation of the drawing with the same name in the chapter "Guarini Reassembled" and is a reference to a specific set of drawings in the unpaginated plates at the end of *Architettura civile*. The second type of example is a distillation of Guarini's techniques. These are limited to the examples in "Deforming the Semicircle" and "The Line." The purpose of these drawings is to distill certain operations presented in "Dell'ortografia gettata" without the added complexity of completing the full projection of a three-dimensional vault.

While this section revisits the drawings from both "Reassembling Guarini" and "Guarini Reassembled," the examination here is technical. It focuses nearly exclusively on the explanation of the geometric techniques deployed in both "Dell'ortografia gettata" and every drawing produced for this book. All the geometric relationships used to produce the drawings in "Guarini Animated" are also described in this chapter. The key difference is that whereas "Guarini Animated" uses code to set out the geometric relationships, they are produced graphically in this chapter. The drawings in this book are one possible reading of Guarini's "Dell'ortografia gettata," and it is assumed that there are many other possibilities. Ultimately, this chapter presents Guarini's orthographic projection as a set of methods that have been and can continue to be modified, adapted, and reconfigured.

Orthographic Projection

The following section provides an overview of some of the basic operations present in "Dell'ortografia gettata." It is a short examination of selected principles and techniques necessary to comprehend and execute Guarini's drawings.

Trattato IV, Lastra I, Figura 1 Explained

The first figure to appear in "Dell'ortografia gettata" is a circle intersected by two lines (FIGURE 7.1).[1] The following is an elaboration of this figure to explain some fundamentals of orthographic projection. There are three drawings in this figure, each comprising a top, front, and side view of a circle. The topmost drawing (FIGURE 7.1A) presents circle *ABCD* cut by two lines: *QT* and *AB*. Because all distances from the center of a circle to its perimeter are equal, and because lines *QT* and *AB* both pass through the center at point *X*, *QT* and *AB* must also be equal. However, when they are projected down onto a plane described by reference line *RL1*, line *QT* is shorter than line *AB*. Line *AB* is perpendicular to the projection lines that move the line onto the plane, and its length is preserved. Therefore, information parallel to the plane of projection is at true length.

The second drawing (FIGURE 7.1B) presents a circle rotated in the right side view. Circle *ABCD* is drawn as solid lines AB and CD in the right side and bottom views, respectively. If line *CD* is rotated about point *X* so that it is no longer vertical, it produces a new diagonal line, *C'D'*. If all points on the original circle are rotated onto line *C'D'* and projected back into the original top view of circle *ABCD*, then line *C'D'* is now shorter than line *CD* in the top view. A curve plotted through points *C'BD'A* produces an ellipse with a minor diameter equal to line *C'D'* and a major diameter equal to line *AB*. Projecting perpendicularly to line *C'D'* produces circle *A'B'C'D'*, which has the same radius as circle *ABCD*. Projecting and rotating this information down into the front view of circle *ABCD*, drawn as line *AB*, produces a different ellipse. While these ellipses can be described as "views" of the original circle *ABCD*, they can also be seen as the products of a proportional operation in which one perpendicular dimension of the circle has been attenuated by projecting between unparallel lines.

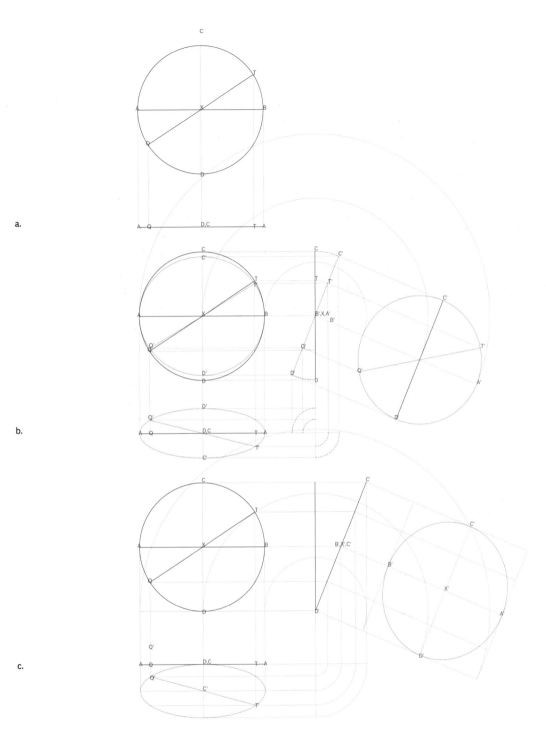

a.

b.

c.

Fig 7.1

The third drawing (FIGURE 7.1C) presents a circle projected onto an inclined plane. Circle *ABCD* is projected to the right until it intersects line *C'D'*. When all points on circle *ABCD* have been projected onto this line and then projected back to the original circle, all dimensions are preserved. However, if perpendicular lines are drawn from line *C'D'*, and distance *AB* is transferred to line *B'A'*, a new ellipse is drawn with major diameter *C'D'* and minor diameter *B'D'*. In the previous example (FIGURE 7.1B), the circle was rotated, and its dimensions were preserved. In this example (FIGURE 7.1C), the original circle has been projected onto an inclined plane and stretched. The new curve, *A'B'C'D'*, is an ellipse linked to the original circle with parallel lines.

The Line

The following operation (FIGURE 7.2) is fundamental to extract the length of lines within a given drawing. It is not explicitly covered as a single operation in "Dell'ortografia gettata," but it is central to many of the observations on conic vaults.[2] It involves rotating a line in two directions. One rotation is parallel to the picture plane, and it appears as an arc; the second rotation is perpendicular to the picture plane, and it appears as a line. The top drawing (FIGURE 7.2A) depicts two projections of line *AB*. Although it is not possible to know the true length of this line from the drawings provided, it is possible to extract the true length of the line through rotation (FIGURE 7.2B). Line *AB* is rotated upward by means of an arc to point *T* that positions it perpendicularly to the projection of lines connecting it to the lower projection. A line is then drawn perpendicularly to line *AT* and downward until it intersects the horizontal projection of *A* at point *T'*. A new line, *BT'*, in the lower projection is the true length of line *AB*.

This can be proven by means of a cone with a center and vertex at point *B* and radius of *AB* (FIGURE 7.2C). A planar section though a cone that begins at diameter *TR* and passes through vertex *B* produces a triangle with a base equal to the diameter of cone *TR* and with sides equal to line *BT*. Any line drawn from vertex *B* to any point on diameter *TR* is the same length as line *BT*. Therefore, line *BT* is the true length of line *AB*.

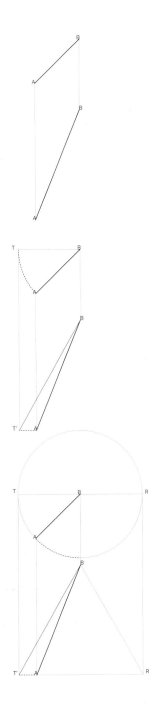

Fig 7.2

Deforming the Semicircle

The following section introduces basic methods of proportionally deforming the semicircle (FIGURES 7.3–7.10). They are based on techniques that Guarini used throughout "Dell'ortografia gettata," although some of them go beyond the examples he provides. At one level, they can be seen as the intersection of the extrusion of a semicircle (i.e., a half cylinder) and another surface. Another option is to understand them purely as two-dimensional deformations. The former asserts one reading of the resultant curves; the latter provides a multitude of readings. The new curve could be a three-dimensionally distorted semicircle shown in one view, or it could be a new two-dimensional planar curve of distended proportions. In any of these options, the link between the semicircle and the resultant distorted curve with parallel lines positions all dimensional control within the simplest of figures: the circle.

Stretching a Semicircle Horizontally

FIGURE 7.3 stretches the horizontal dimensions of a semicircle by rotating and extending the reference line. Reference Line RL0 is rotated downward to an angle less than ninety degrees to produce reference line RL1. Point A of the original semicircle, AEI, is projected downward until it intersects reference line RL1. All other points on semicircle AEI are then projected perpendicularly from line RL0 to line RL1. The vertical dimensions from RL2 are rotated until they intersect vertical reference line RL3. These points are then projected parallel to line RL1. The inter-section of points A–H with reference line RL1 are

projected perpendicularly to reference line RL3 until they intersect their corresponding projection from reference line RL1. This operation preserves vertical dimensions while stretching horizontal ones. The principal operation is a direct implementation of Euclid's intercept theorem in which proportional relationships between intersecting lines are preserved when connected with parallel projectors.[3]

Shearing a Semicircle

FIGURE 7.4 builds on the horizontal elongation of the semicircle from the previous example. However, instead of projecting perpendicularly to reference RL1 to locate the points on the new curve, the points are projected perpendicularly to reference line RL0. This results in a sheared grid of lines in which the grid's internal angles do not equal ninety degrees. Plotting the curve within this grid results in a sheared version of the original semicircle. The new curve is equal in height to the original semicircle, but it has been asymmetrically stretched along the horizontal axis.

Stretching the Semicircle along a Line

FIGURE 7.5 stretches the vertical dimensions of the semicircle along a line. Vertical reference line RL1 is rotated downward by an angle less than ninety degrees to produce a new reference line, RL2. All points on the original semicircle are then projected parallel to reference line RL0 until they intersect line R2. The points of intersection with reference line RL2 are then projected downward vertically until they intersect line RL0. These intersections are then rotated back until they intersect reference line RL1. The intersection of

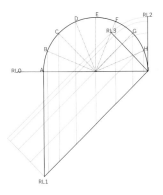

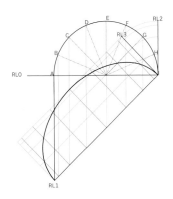

Fig 7.3

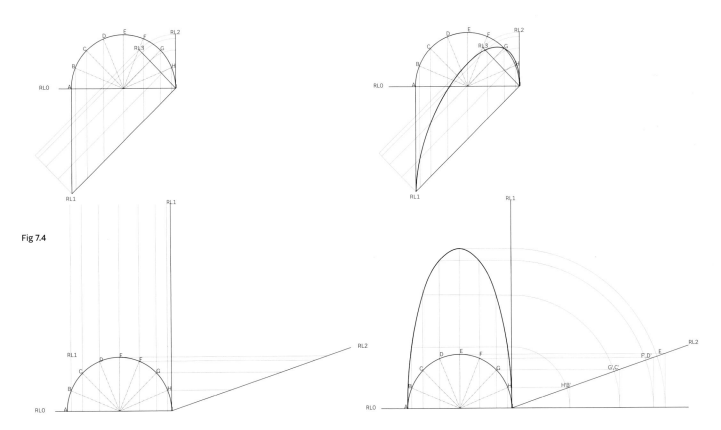

Fig 7.4

Fig 7.5

the arcs of rotation and reference line *RL1* are then projected parallel to line *RL0*. Points *A–I* are projected perpendicular to reference line *RL0* until they intersect the projections from reference line *RL1*. The curve is then plotted within this grid.

Projecting a Semicircle onto a Sphere

FIGURE 7.6 depends on finding the radius of the circular section through the sphere at the point of intersection. All sections through a sphere are circles; therefore, once the circle has been drawn in the top view, the points of intersection can be located on the projection line. Point *X* is the center of a sphere with radius *XI*. Points *A–I* on arc *AEI* are projected parallel to reference line *RL0* until they intersect the curve defined by radius *XI*. The distance between the points of intersection from reference line *RL1* provides the radius on the horizontal section through the sphere. Thus, points *G'* and *C'* lie on an arc with a radius equal to the distance from *G'* or *C'* to reference line *RL1*. Projecting point *X* to reference line *RL0* and rotating it until it intersects reference line *RL2* locates the point in the top projection. Projecting it horizontally (i.e., parallel to reference line *RL0*) until it intersects the vertical projection of point *E* locates the sphere in

the top view. Each of the radii defined by the points of intersection can then be drawn from point *X*, and the intersection with the corresponding points from the original arc with these radii provides the points on a new curve, *A'E'I'*, in the top view.

Projecting a Semicircle onto a Cone

FIGURE 7.7 depends on finding the radius of the circular sections through the cone at the points of intersection. All planar sections through a right cone— sections parallel to the cone's base—are circles. Line *IV* is half the vertical planar section through a cone with a center at point *X* and a vertex at point *V*. The projection of points *G* and *C* onto line *IV* are *G'* and *C'*. The perpendicular distance from line *XV* and points *G'* and *C'* defines the radius of the circular planar section on which points *G'* and *C'* must lie. Rotating point *X* from the side view into the top view and then drawing an arc with a radius equal to the perpendicular distance from line *XV* to point *G'* or *C'* describes the planar section through the cone in the top view. Projecting points *G* and *C* from the original semicircle onto this arc locates points *G'* and *C'* in the top view. The remainder of the points on a new curve, *A'E'C'*, can be plotted in the same manner.

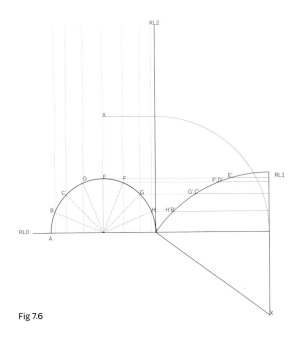

Fig 7.6

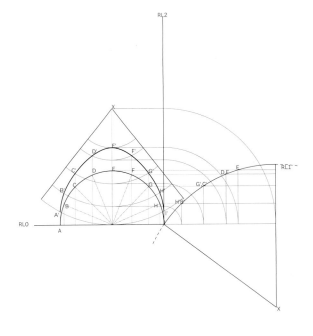

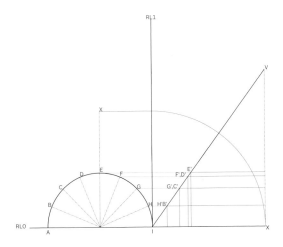

Fig 7.7

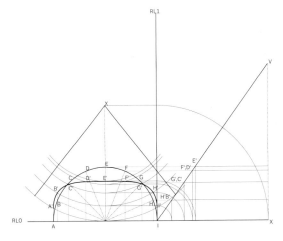

Projecting a Semicircle at an Inclined Angle onto a Cone

FIGURE 7.8 depends on plotting the elliptical sections through the cone at the points of intersection. This projection combines Guarini's method for plotting the projection of a semicircle onto an oblique cylinder[4] and a cone.[5] Given the front view and half top view of cone *IVP* with a center at point *X* and semicircle *AEI* oriented on diagonal line *AI*, each point on semicircle *AEI* is projected through cone *IVP* parallel to line *AI*. The projections of points *A* and *I* (i.e., *A'* and *I'*) must lie on the planar section through the cone defined by line *I9*. The planar section is through a closed surface (i.e., a cone) and therefore must result in a closed curve. Because this line is not parallel to the base of cone *IVP* it cannot be a circle. The ellipse is the other planar section through a cone that results in a closed curve in finite space.[6] Therefore, points *A'* and *I'* must lie on an ellipse. To plot the ellipse, the intersections of line *I9* with the ruling lines of cone *IVP* (e.g., line *VM*) are plotted and labeled *I, 2, 3, 4, 5, 6, 7, 8,* and *9*. Each point is then rotated to reference line *RL2* and projected parallel to reference line *RL0*. Points *I, 2, 3, 4, 5, 6, 7, 8,* and *9* are then plotted in the top view by projecting parallel to the axis of the cone (line *A1,5*) until they intersect the corresponding ruling line. Therefore, point *4* is projected parallel to the axis of the cone until it intersects line *VL*.

Point *5* must be found by locating it on a circular section through the cone because ruling line *XX* is parallel in the top and bottom views. This can be accomplished by projecting point *5* parallel to the base of the cone until it intersects line *VP* at point *R*. Point *R* is projected parallel to the axis of the cone until it intersects the base of the cone, line *IP*. The point of intersection is then rotated until it intersects line *VX* at point *5*. The curve plotted through these points is the view of the elliptical section perpendicular to line *IP*. Transferring these distances symmetrically about point *T* and projecting them perpendicularly until they intersect the projections of points *I, 2, 3, 4, 5, 6, 7, 8,* and *9* results in the plotting of the elliptical section through cone *IVP*. In this example, only a portion of the ellipse has been drawn for clarity.

The last portion of the projection involves plotting the remaining points of intersection on the ruling lines of the cone. The perpendicular projection of point *V* to line *I9* is the location of point *V* in the top view. Rotating this projection to reference line *RL1* and projecting it horizontally until it intersects the perpendicular projection of point *T* locates point *V* in the top view.[7] Furthermore, the ruling lines of the cone can be plotted by connecting the numbered points on the elliptical curve to point *V* in the top view. The points of intersection with each planar section through the cone can be rotated upward to reference line *RL2* and then projected perpendicularly until they intersect the corresponding ruling line of the cone. Completing this operation for each planar section results in plotting the elliptical conic sections at all points of intersection. The last step is to project upward from the original semicircle, *AEI*, until each points of the original semicircle is connected to the corresponding elliptical section. Once these points have been plotted. The curve can be drawn through them.

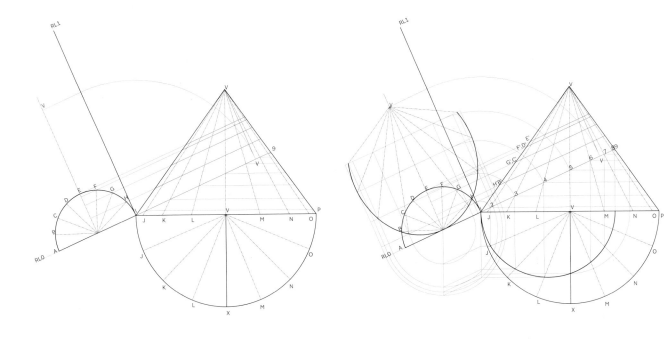

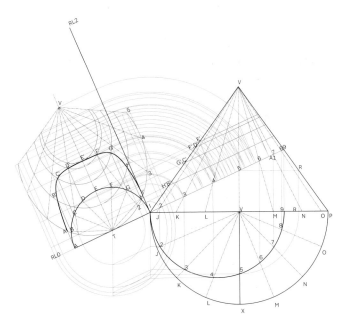

Fig 7.8

Projecting a Semicircle onto a Surface of Revolution

FIGURE 7.9 is not covered in Guarini's "Dell'ortografia gettata," but it is based on his projections for cones, spheres, and cylinders. A surface of revolution is a surface generated by rotating a planar curve around an axis lying in the plane of the curve.[8] Therefore, a section taken perpendicularly to the plane of revolution is a circle. This makes the problem like that of a cone. The projection of points *H* and *B* of the semicircle *AEI* onto curve *IV* results in points *H'* and *B'*. The distance from these points to the axis of revolution (i.e., line *XV*) provides the radius of the circular section on which they must lie. Transferring this radius to point *X* in the top view and then drawing a circle results in plotting the planar sections through surface *IV* at points *H'* and *B'*. Projecting points *H* and *B* from the original semicircle vertically until they intersect the previously drawn circle results in the plotting of points *H'* and *B'* in the top view. The remaining points on a new curve, *A'E'I'*, can be plotted in the same manner.

Projecting a Semicircle onto a Torus

Guarini did cover the geometric description of the torus, but he did not cover the projection of a semicircle onto a torus (FIGURE 7.10).[9] A torus is created by rotating a circle (i.e., a planar curve) about an axis on the same plane as the circle. It is therefore a surface of revolution and can be solved in the same manner. The torus in this example is defined by semicircle *IMP* and the axis of revolution, line *VX*. The projection of points *H* and *B* of the semicircle *AEI* onto semicircle *IMP* results in points *H'* and *B'*. The distance from these points to the axis of revolution (i.e., line *XV*) provides the radius of the circular section on which points *H'* and *B'* must lie. Transferring this radius to point *X* in the top view and then drawing a circle results in plotting the planar sections through the torus at points *H'* and *B'*. Projecting points *H* and *B* from the original semicircle vertically until they intersect the previously drawn circle results in the plotting of points *H'* and *B'* in the top view. The remaining points of a new curve, *A'E'I'*, on the torus can be plotted in the same manner.

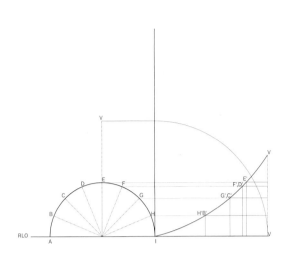

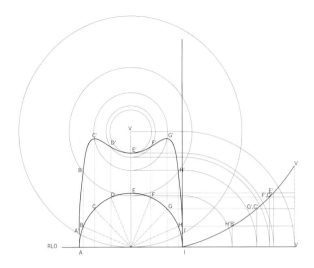

Fig 7.9

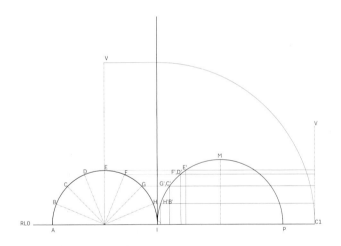

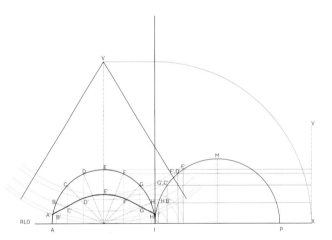

Fig 7.10

The Vaults

The following section focuses on the explanation of seven vaults taken directly from "Dell' ortografia gettata." Each explanation is sequential, presenting the drawings and procedures as sets of operations conducted over time. Furthermore, an endnote for every explanation provides the pagination for Guarini's original textual description. The explanations provide information on both Guarini's original instructions and the means by which they were reconstructed for this book.

Trattato IV, Lastra II, Figure 1–3 Explained

Much of "Dell'ortografia gettata" centers on the generation of different vault forms through the projection of a semicircle onto an array of surfaces. It is not surprising that Guarini's first example of the orthographic projection of a vault is a semicircular arch projected onto curved and folded surfaces.[10] The following example has been expanded to include a cone, an inclined plane, and their side projections (FIGURE 7.11). Semicircular arch *ABC* is projected downward with parallel lines to line *LM*. An arc (i.e., *HBR*) is drawn through the projection lines so that it intersects every line. The points of intersection with arc *HBR* and the vertical projection (e.g., points *B*, *7*, and *8*) are projected parallel to reference line *RL1* until they intersect line *CM* and are then rotated about point *C* until they intersect horizontal reference line *RL1*. They are also projected perpendicularly and then upward from reference line *RL1* until they intersect their corresponding horizontal projection from the original line. Therefore, the vertical projection of point *8* intersects the horizontal projection of point *8* from the original arch, *ABC*. Plotting all the points of intersection results in side view *BEFR*. The same operation can be used to plot the elevations of folded plane *IBQ* and curve *JBP*.

The last two intersections on this page require additional explanation. The projections involve a conic surface and an inclined plane. Line *KBN* is the profile line of a cone with an axis of *LM*.[11] Thus, point *N* lies on the base of the cone. Because the cone's axis is set, line *LM*, perpendicular to line *CM*, sections through the cone parallel to line *CM* are circles. These circles appear as lines in the top view, but in the elevation on reference line *RL1*, they are circles and can be used to plot the intersection of the cone. Following this logic, point *N* lies on a circle centered at point *M*. Rotating points *N* and *M* about point *C* until they intersect reference line *RL1* repositions these points in the side projection. Drawing an arc centered on point *M* and through point *N* locates point *N* on the reference line. Similarly, if point *8* on line *KN* is rotated about point *C* until it intersects reference line *RL1*, the radius of the circle on which point *8* lies is now located in the elevation projection. Drawing an arc centered on point *M* through point *8* on line *RL1* provides the circular segment on which point *8* must lie in elevation. Therefore, point *8* on the original arch, *ABC*, is projected horizontally until it intersects radius *M8*. The newly plotted point *8* is the side projection of point *8* on a cone with a center at point *M*. All other points of this intersection can be plotted in the same manner.

The last example is the inclined plane.[12] It begins in the side projection with the drawing of a diagonal line beginning at point *M* and ending when it intersects the horizontal projection of point *B*. This is the edge view of an inclined plane. The intersection of the horizontal projections (e.g., points *5* and *1*) with line *MB* are projected downward to reference line *RL1* and then rotated about point *C* until they intersect line *CM*. The intersections with line *CM* are then projected horizontally (i.e., parallel to reference line *RL0*) until they intersect the corresponding vertical projection. Therefore, point *5* is located when its projection

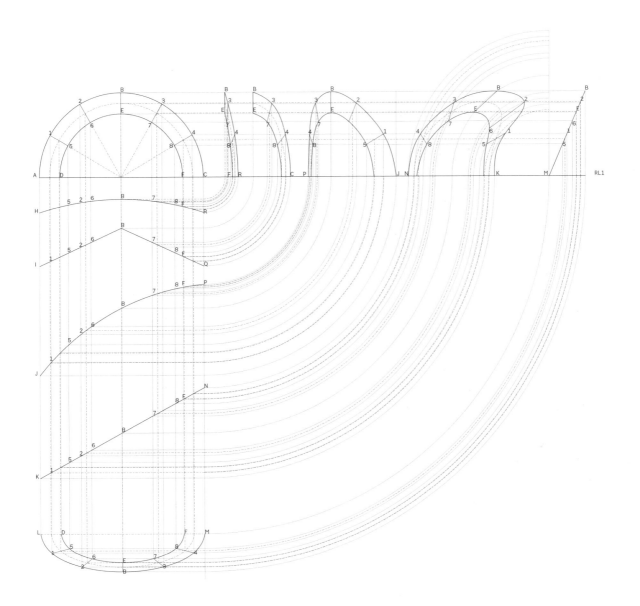

Fig 7.11

from the side intersects the vertical projection of point 5 from the original semicircular arch, *ABC*. The remainder of the points for plotting inclined arc *LBM* can be found by repeating the same steps for each point. These operations work because, regardless of what the semicircle is projected onto, its original dimensional properties of height and width are unchanged. This makes the projection reversible.

The complete projection of a vault requires all its faces to be drawn flat on the picture plane so that their true proportional dimensions can be obtained (FIGURE 7.12). Because all operations are based on the original semicircular arch, *ABC*, many of the important dimensional properties needed to flatten the vault are present in this drawing. To begin, the distance from point *C* to point 4 on arch *ABC* is rotated about point *C* until it intersects reference line *RL1*. This is the dimension of one segment of the arch, and it is the same for every projection. Distance *C4* is then transferred horizontally along reference line *RL2* six times (one for each joint) and then projected perpendicularly to reference line *RL1* until they intersect reference line *RL2*. This plots points *C'*, *4'*, *3'*, *B'*, *2'*, *1'*, and *A'*. The points of intersection on curve *HBR* and folded plane *IBQ* are then projected horizontally until they intersect the corresponding vertical line, such that point 4 lies on the vertical line beginning at point *4'*, and point 3 lies on the vertical line beginning at point *3'*. Plotting all points provides the unrolled outer surface of vault *HRQI*, approximated with planes.

The next step involves plotting the joints between the subdivisions of arch *ABC* (e.g., lines *8,4* and *7,3*). Distance *CF* is transferred to each point plotted on reference line *RL2*. All joints have the same dimensions, so this distance can be used to plot points *F'*, *8'*, *7'*, *E'*, *5'*, *6'*, and *D'*. Vertical lines are then constructed

perpendicularly to reference line *RL2* from these points. The points of intersection on curve *HBR* and folded plane *IBQ* are projected horizontally until they intersect their corresponding vertical line, such that point 8 lies on the vertical line beginning at point *8'*, and point 7 lies on the vertical line beginning at point *7'*. Plotting all points provides the unrolled joints of vault *HRQI*. The process described above can be followed for curve *JBP* and inclined arch *LBM*.

The vault that is intersected by a cone could be unrolled directly from the side projection. However, for consistency, it is unrolled from the top view. This projection requires an additional step: it must first be projected back downward in the top view of the vault and then unrolled.[13] The points on curve *NBK* in the side projection are projected down perpendicularly to reference line *RL1*. The intersections with *RL1* are then rotated about point *C* until they intersect line *CM*. The intersections with line *CM* are then projected horizontally (i.e., parallel to reference line *RL1*) until they intersect the corresponding vertical projection of arch *ABC*, such that the horizontal projection of point 4 intersects the vertical projection of point 4. All other points on the curve can be plotted in the same manner. Once the points have been plotted and the curve has been drawn, vault *KNML* can be unrolled in the same manner as for vault *HRQI*.

The completed drawing connects all the vaults as a single unrolled cylindrical barrel vault with irregular seams. This foregrounds the relationship between the original source arch, *ABC*, and its projected variations. Guarini explained this principle by accompanying the orthographic projection with an illustration depicting each projection as different cuts from the same hollow stone cylinder.[14]

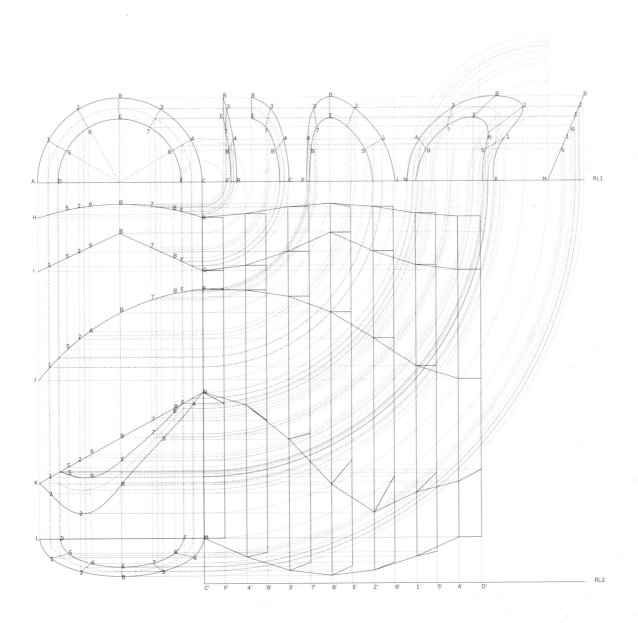

Fig 7.12

Trattato IV, Lastra IV, Figure 4–5 Explained

Six of the fourteen plates associated with the fourth tractate are dedicated to barrel vaults. The example explained here deals with the projection of an oblique arch onto a cone.[15] It begins with projecting semicircular arch *ABC* onto an inclined and oblique plane (FIGURE 7.13). The points on arch *ABC* are projected perpendicularly to reference line *RL0* until they intersect line *LK*. Diagonal line *LM* is then drawn, setting the oblique angle of the vault in plan. Distance *KM* is transferred to point *C*, and then an arc is drawn. A line is drawn from point *A* to a point tangent to the previously drawn arc. This locates point *P* and establishes line *CP*. Lines parallel to line *AP* are constructed from the projection of each point on arch *ABC* onto reference line *RL0*. Therefore, point *1* on arch *ABC* is projected downward to reference line *RL0* and parallel to line *AP* until it intersects line *CP*, producing point *1'*. A line is then drawn parallel to line *AP*, beginning at point *C*. Its intersection with the arc of radius *CP*, producing point *A'*. Line *CA'* is drawn and then all points of intersection located on *NP* are rotated until they intersect line *CA'*.

Returning to the original semicircular arch, *ABC*: point *B* is projected parallel to reference line *RL0* until it intersects reference line *RL1* (FIGURE 7.13). This point is then rotated until it intersects the extension of line *PC* at point *R*, producing line segment *CR*. This process is repeated for every point on arch *ABC* until all points are located on line *CR*. The angle between line *CR* and reference line *RL1* is now equal to angle *CAP*. To locate point *B'* on the new oblique arch, *B1* is projected upward from line *CA'* parallel to line *RL1*

until it intersects the projection of *B* on line *CR*, which is parallel to line *CA'*. Every point on the arch can be found in this manner, producing the side view of the skewed arch. The side view is the end product, but much of the operation is contingent upon plotting similar versions of triangle *LKM* without reference to perceptual space.

A normal view is perpendicular to the object being drawn. It conveys proportionally accurate dimensional information. To obtain the normal view of oblique arch *A'B'C*, Guarini instructed the reader to transfer the distance from *A'U* from the side view to a line drawn perpendicularly to point *M*, locating point *T* (FIGURE 7.14). Line *LT* is sloping ground line *CA'* in the side view, drawn at true length. The distances from line *CA'* to points on arch *A'B'C* are taken perpendicularly to reference line *RL0* and are then transferred to lines drawn perpendicularly to line *LM* from the intersection with the vertical projection from arch *ABC*. Point *B'''* can be found by constructing a line perpendicular to line *LM* at point *B*. The intersection of this line with line *LT* (i.e., at point *B'*) can be used as the base point to transfer distance *B1,B'* from the side view, locating point *B'''*. Every point in the normal view can be found in this manner.[16]

The second part of this projection is the intersection of the vault with a cone (FIGURE 7.15). To begin, a line is drawn at any angle across the vertical projections of arch *ABC* (e.g., line *XZ*). Let line *XZ* describe the intersection of a cone with a plane originating at axis *LK* and parallel to the picture plane. This makes line *XZ* the true length of a line drawn from the vertex of the cone to its base at *LZ*. Furthermore, because all projections from arch *ABC* are perpendicular to line *LK*,

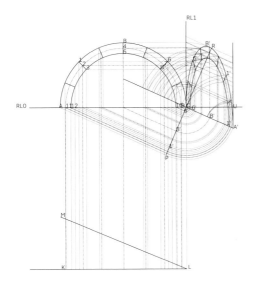

Fig 7.13

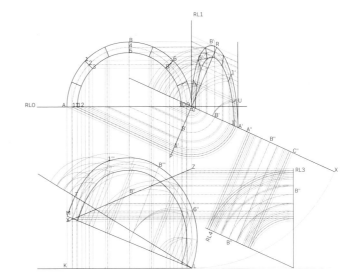

Fig 7.15

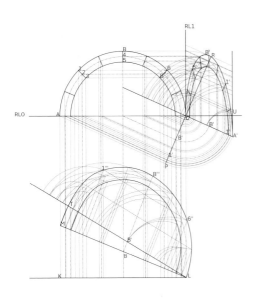

Fig 7.14

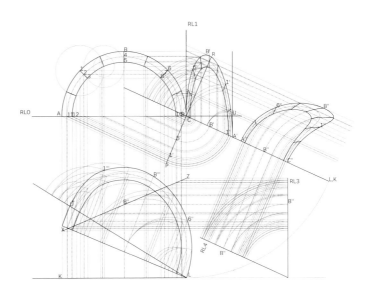

Fig 7.16

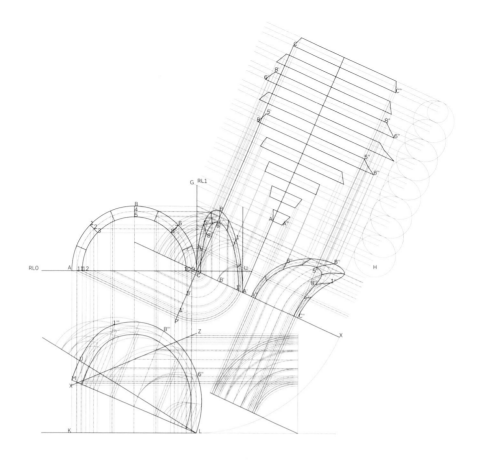

Fig 7.17

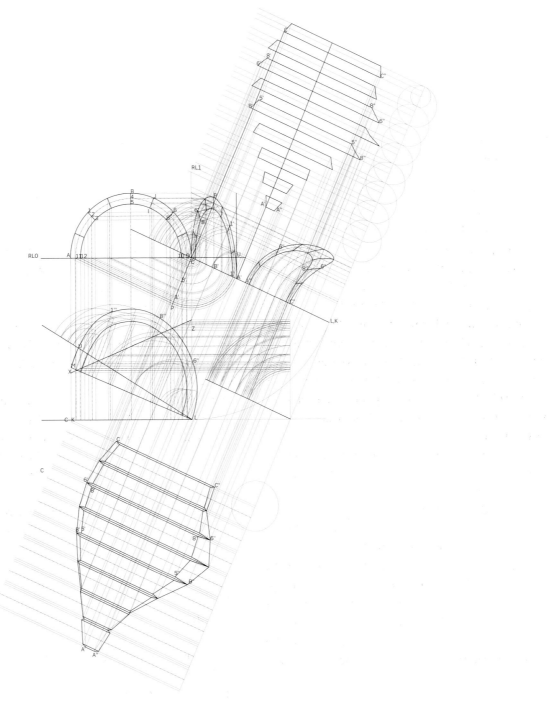

Fig 7.18

sections through the cone at the point of intersection with line *XZ* are circles. All perpendicular distances from lines *XZ* and *LK* are transferred via projection to line *CX* through rotation and projection. Point *V* on line *CV* represents the end view of line *LK* and the center point of the cone described by line *XZ*.

To plot the side view of the intersection of point *B″*, the intersection of the vertical projection (perpendicular to line *RL0*) of point *B* on arch *ABC* is located on line *XZ* at point *B″* (FIGURE 7.16). This point is then projected parallel to line *LK* until it intersects reference line *RL3*, and then it is rotated back to *RL4*, setting it parallel to line *CV*. Point *B″* is then located on line *CX* by projecting it perpendicularly to reference line *RL4*. An arc drawn through point *B″* on line *CX* and centered at point *V* produces the planar section through the cone on which *B″* must lie. The intersection of this arc with the projection of point *B″* on oblique arch *ABC* and parallel to line *CX* locates point *B″* on conic arch *A″B″C″*. All points on conic arch *A″B″C″* can be found in this manner.

Once both arches have been drawn in the side view, the vault can be unrolled (FIGURE 7.17). The projections of arches *A′B′C′* and *A″B″C″* on line *CV* are not perpendicular to the picture plane. However, the lines parallel to line *CV* that connect the arches are. These lines describe the cylindrical surfaces that connects arch *A′B′C′* to arch *A″B″C″*. Therefore, line *B′B″* is parallel to the picture plane and at a true proportional length. In addition, because the original semicircular arch, *ABC*, is described as line *CR* in the side view, its normal view is perpendicular to the projection plane. Therefore, its properties can be used to unroll the vault.

Line *B5* in arch *ABC* is a joint between two pieces of stone or paper. The arch and the vault are therefore divided into eight pieces. All joints in arch *ABC* have the same depth as *B5* because arch *ABC* is a semicircle, and the joints are segments of the radii. Because the dimensions of arch *ABC* are rotated onto line *CR*, they have not been distorted. This means that distance *B5* can be used to unroll the vault. This distance is used to create a set of lines parallel to line *CV* (e.g., line *HG*). Each joint is then projected perpendicularly from line *CV* until they intersect the corresponding perpendicular line. Points *B′*, *B″*, *5′*, and *5″* are projected upward to describe the shape of joint *B′B″5″5′*. All other joints can be found in this manner.

In a similar manner, the top and bottom surfaces of the vault can be unrolled in relationship to one another from the side view (FIGURE 7.18). Distance *BJ* is the distance between all joints on the outer surface of the vault. Therefore, a set of lines can be constructed parallel to line *CV*, using this distance as a guide. Distance *5I* can then be used to construct another set of lines centered between the previous set, describing the unrolled inner surface of the cylinder. Points on the arches (e.g., *1′1″*, *3′*, and *3″*) can be projected downward perpendicularly to line *CX*. When all points on the arches have been located, the unrolled vault is drawn.

Trattato IV, Lastra VIII, Figure 4–6 Explained

The following projections are for a conic vault truncated by an inclined plane.[17] Guarini's method for developing a conic vault begins with the circle, as it did with his studies of barrel vaults. However, unlike the drawings of barrel vaults, the drawing of a conic vault depends on rotating the ruling lines of the conic surface. The ruling lines of a cone extend from its vertex to its base, and in a right cone with a circular base, the lengths of every ruling line on the surface of the cone is the same. The projection begins with a quadrant of circle *AB* (FIGURE 7.19). The points on quarter arc *AB* are projected downward to a horizontal line (i.e., line *G1B*). Lines are then constructed to connect the points of intersection (i.e., *B*, *2*, *1*, and *A*) on line *G1B* with point *G2* to describe the outer surface of the cone. Point *G3* is found by drawing a line from point *D*, which is parallel to line *BG2*, until it intersects line *G1G2*. Once point *G3* is located, inner quarter arc *CD* is also projected downward to horizontal line *G1B*, and the points of intersection (i.e., *C*, *D*, *3*, and *4*) are connected to point *G3* with lines. This creates the side view of conic vault *BG1G2* composed of two cones with parallel surfaces.

The next step involves slicing the conic vault with an inclined plane (FIGURE 7.20). Points *G2* and *G3* are projected parallel to line *G1B* until they intersect a vertical line (parallel to line *G1G2*) drawn from point *Q*. This locates the vertices of the conic vault in the top view. The horizontal dimensions of the original quarter arch are then transferred symmetrically about point *Q*. The intersections of the transferred dimensions of the outer arch and line *G1B* are then connected to point *G2*. The inner arch dimensions are connected to point *G3*. This locates the ruling lines of the cone in the top view. To cut the cone, a diagonal line is drawn at any angle less than ninety degrees relative to line *G1b* from point *G1*. The intersections with this line and every line passing through both points *G2* and *G3* are then projected parallel to line *G1B* until they intersect the corresponding ruling line of the cone. Therefore,

point *S* lies on ruling line *G3,3* in the side view. Point *S* is projected horizontally (parallel to line *G1B*) until it intersects line *G3,3* in the top view at point *S*. The remaining points on the curve can be located in the same manner.

To construct a normal view of the planar cut through the cone, the points of intersection with line *G1Z* are rotated until they intersect line *G1A*. These points are then projected parallel to line *G1A* until they intersect their corresponding perpendicular projection from the top view. Point *Z* is rotated from line *G1Z* to line *G1A* and projected horizontally until it intersects the perpendicular projection of point *Z* in the top view. All other points on the normal view of curve *JZH* can be found in the same manner.

Guarini's conic vault is composed of pieces. Regardless of whether these pieces are made of stone or paper, or even if they remain depictions in pixels or ink, each piece has five sides. Therefore, in the top view, points *U*, *V*, *N*, *Z*, *G2*, and *G3* define the boundaries of a solid that is one piece of the conic vault (FIGURE 7.21). To build the conic vault, the true proportional dimensions of each side must be drawn. To begin, the interior surface of the conic vault is unrolled through rotation about point *G3*.[18] In the uncut cone, all ruling lines are the same length. Therefore, line *G3Y*, which is drawn parallel to the picture plane, is at true length. Line *G3Y* is also the true length of every ruling line on the inner surface of the conic vault before it was cut with line *G1Z*.

Distance *2D4* on the interior arc of the original quarter arch is the linear distance between points *2D* and *4* along the quarter arc. Because the quarter arc has been equally divided, and because the curvature of a circle is constant, the length of every segment is equal to distance *2D4*. Therefore, rotating point *Y* about point *G3* until it intersects reference line *RL2* locates one ruling line of the cone along a base line. Transferring distance *2D4* along the arc generated by radius *G3Y* locates the end point of the next ruling line. Repeating this process three times provides one quarter of the uncut conic vault so that triangle *C3'G3* comprises one interior face of the uncut conic vault.

To locate the cut on the unrolled pieces of the interior vault, the points on curve *JZH* must be projected to line *G3Y* and rotated about *G3* until they intersect their corresponding ruling line. Therefore, point *X* is projected parallel to line *JH* until it intersects line *G3Y*. The distance from the point of intersection to point *G3* is the true length of line *G3X*. To locate point *X* on the unrolled surface, it must be rotated until it intersects line *G3,4'* at point *X'*. The location the vault is bilaterally symmetrical, only half of the vault must be unrolled.

To draw the exterior ruling lines of the conic vault in relation to interior ruling lines, Guarini began by drawing a line parallel to line *G3Y'* at a distance equal to the distance between the interior and exterior surfaces of the vault (FIGURE 7.22). This distance is found by drawing a line through point *G3* that is perpendicular to line *G2B*. This new line, *G3W*, is the perpendicular distance between the interior and exterior surface of the conical vault. Line *G2'A'* is then constructed parallel line *G3Y'* at a perpendicular distance of *G3H*. Point *G2* is rotated about point *G3* until it intersects line *G2'H'* at point *G2'*. Point *H* is rotated about point *G2* until it is parallel with line *G2'H'*. Distance *G2H* is transferred to point *G2'* and rotated until it intersects the parallel offset of line *G3Y'* at point *H'*. Polygon *Y'H'G2G3* is the proportionally accurate shape and size of one joint within the conic vault. The remaining joints can be found in the same manner.

In "Dell'ortografia gettata," Guarini provided a drawing that represents each vault as an unrolled set of stones lying on the outer surface of the vault. This drawing provides the accurate proportional shape and size of the interior face (i.e., *intrado*) and the exterior face (i.e., *extrado*) of each stone within the vault. To complete this drawing with the conic vault, the same process can be followed by unrolling the exterior surface about point *G2* (FIGURE 7.23). Distance *G2* is rotated about point *G2* to locate point *G2H"*.[19] Distance *B2* is the linear distance between each point along the exterior face of uncut conical vault *BAG2*. This distance, *B2*, is transferred along the circumference of the arc defined by radius *G2H"*. This locates points *B'*, *2'*, *1'*, and *H"*. The unrolled ruling lines of the cone's exterior surface are then drawn by connecting points *B'*, *2'*, *1'*, and *H"* with point *G2*. These triangles describe the unrolled exterior surfaces of the cone before they are cut.

Point *G3* is rotated about point *G2* until it intersects each centerline in the unrolled surfaces, thereby locating the same point in each of the unrolled pieces. Distances *4'Y'*, *4',3'*, and *3'C'* from the unrolled interior surface are then transferred to the center of the corresponding segment of the unrolled exterior cone. Therefore, distance *4'Y'* is centered between points *H'* and *2'*; distance *4'3'* is centered between points *2'* and *1'*; and distance *3'C'* is centered between points *1'* and *A'*. Drawing lines from each of the newly located points to points *G3a*, *G3b*, and *G3c* describes the interior surface of the uncut conical vault in relation to the exterior. To locate the cut in the outer surface, point *M* in the top

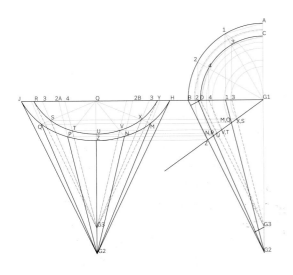

Fig 7.19

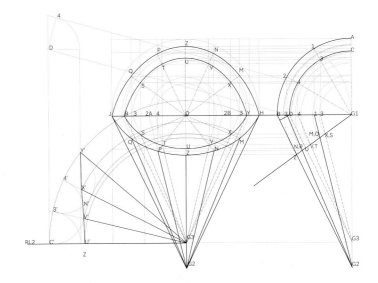

Fig 7.21

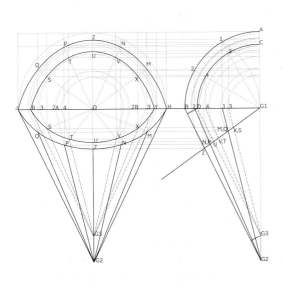

Fig 7.20

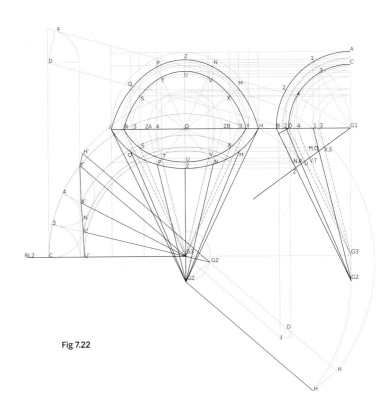

Fig 7.22

view is projected horizontally until it intersects line *G2H* and then is rotated about point *G2* until it intersects line *G2,1* at point *M"*. The same process can be used to locate points *N"* and *Z"*.

The cuts on the inner surface of the vault can be found by transferring the distances from the unrolled interior surface described in FIGURE 7.21 to the unrolled exterior surface of the conic vault. To begin, construct a line from point *G3* in the top view of the cone that is parallel to line *G2H"* in the unrolled surface of the cone (FIGURE 7.24). This creates line *G3G*. Next, rotate distance *G3U'* until it intersects this new line and then draw a line from *G3* in the top view to *G3c* in the unrolled surface. Copy this line to the point of intersection of arch *G3U'* with the new parallel line. This transfers distance *G3U'* into the unrolled view, locating point *U"*. Completing the same process for the remaining points locates every point on the unrolled interior surfaces and provides all dimensional information necessary to construct a model of truncated conic vault *G2HJ*.

Trattato IV, Lastra IX, Figure 4–7 Explained

This example explains Guarini's method for unrolling a conoid vault.[20] In a cone, all the lines of the surface converge at a single point. In a conoid, all the lines of the surface converge on a single line of convergence. Guarini began the projection by constructing a quarter arch and projecting it downward to create the side view of a semicone with a vertex at point *H* and half of its base at line *31C* (FIGURE 7.25). Since this figure is a conoid in the side view, point *H* is the exterior

line of convergence, and point *K* is the interior line of convergence. These points are then projected perpendicularly to reference line *RL3* to establish the lines of convergence in the top view. The horizontal distances from point *G* to each point on the quarter arch are then transferred symmetrically about point *31* in the top view, by means of concentric arcs. Therefore, the horizontal distance (parallel to reference line *RL1*) is transferred from point *G* to points *34* and *34'*. Once each of these points on top of quarter arch *31SG* have been located, they are then projected parallel to reference line *RL2* until they intersect line of convergence *HH'*. These lines locate the outer surface of the conoid in the top view. The same process can be repeated to locate the inner surface of the conoid in the top view. These lines represent a conoid with an outer surface that extends from a plane originating at reference line *RL1* and terminating at line of convergence *HH'*.

Guarini then truncated the conoid with two cylinders (FIGURE 7.25). The first cylinder cuts the conoid in the side view with the arc at points *31, 34, 37,* and *40*. The second cylinder cuts the conoid in the side view with the arc at points *41, 44, 47,* and *50*. Each point of intersection is projected parallel to reference line *RL1* until they intersect the corresponding perpendicular projection. Therefore, point *34* is projected parallel to reference line *RL1* until it intersects the projection of point *34* parallel to reference line *RL2*. This locates point *34* in the top view. Because the conoid is bilaterally symmetrical about its axis, point *34* can be mirrored about line *31,41* to locate point *34'*. The same process can be used to locate every point on curve *40'37'34'31,34,37,40'*. Repeating this process with the three remaining curvilinear intersections between

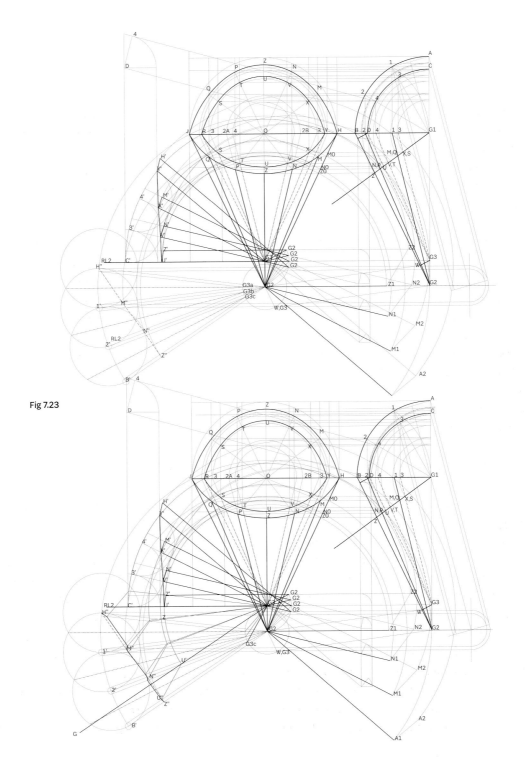

Fig 7.23

Fig 7.24

the cylinders and conoid describes Guarini's truncated conoid in two views.

To obtain the unrolled projection of the intersection of the conoid with a cylinder at curve *31,34,37,40*, Guarini instructed the reader to produce a geometric error (FIGURE 7.26). As was explained in the process of unrolling a barrel vault (FIGURE 7.12), a cylinder can be unrolled by measuring the distances between a set number of divisions of the generating circle and then transferring them to the plane as a set of parallel lines. This process approximates the circumference of the circle with chords of equal length. The same process can be followed to unroll the intersection of the conoid and the cylinder at arc *31,34,37,40*. However, Guarini described a different method that results in a distortion. His text instructs the reader to transfer all the distances from a common point.[21] In Guarini's original, the point is *L*; in this reconstruction, it is point *31*.

Distance *31,34* is transferred to a distance that originates at that projection of point *34* on reference line *RL1* and extends perpendicularly to terminate at point *34*. Distance *31,37* is transferred to a distance that originates at the projection of point *37* on reference *RL1* and extends perpendicularly to terminate at point *37*. And distance *31,40* is transferred to a distance that originates at the projection of point *31* on reference line *RL1* and extends perpendicularly to terminate at point *31*. This describes curve *31,34,37,40* as projected perpendicularly to reference line *RL1*. Importantly, each distance is approximated with a chord of greater length, creating a very subtly distorted version of the intersection. Curve *31,34'37'40'* can be found by mirroring the original curve about line *31,31*. This

means that the difference between the length of chord *40,37* is closer in length to corresponding arc segment *37,40* than chord *40,31* is to corresponding arc segment *40,31*. This discrepancy is small, however, and because Guarini did not use this curve to produce the unrolled templates, its lack of accuracy has no impact on the overall accuracy of the vault's development. In addition, because the discrepancy is so small, it is impossible to know if a different method was used in the construction of the drawing than the method explained in the text.

On a right cone, the true length is the same for every ruling line that passes through the vertex and intersects its circular base. However, because they converge at a point, there is no view that shows all ruling lines at true proportional length. Conversely, the ruling lines on the surface of a conoid are not the same length. Nevertheless, if, as in Guarini's conoid, all ruling lines are parallel in top view, then the true length of every line on the surface of the conoid can be taken from the side view. To begin, Guarini unrolled the uncut conoid, using it as a base on which to plot the intersections with the two cylinders (FIGURE 7.27). Reference line *RL4* is used as the base line for the unrolling. Point *K1* is located on reference line *RL4* at the perpendicular projection of point *31*, which is the centerline of the conoid. Distance *KE* in the side view is transferred to point *K1* on reference line *RL4* perpendicularly to produce point *E'*. Line *K1E'* is the unrolled line at the center of the interior conoidal surface. To find point *U'* in the unrolled projection, distance *EU* is transferred as a circle with radius *EU* to point *E'*. Point *K2* is located on reference line *RL4* by projecting point *32* on reference line *RL1* perpendicularly until it intersects reference line *RL4*. Points *K1* and *K2* are the points of intersection with the ruling lines of the interior surface and line of convergence *KK'*. Distance *KU* is then transferred to point *K2* as the radius of an arc. When this arc intersects the circle created by radius *EU* at *E'*, point *U'* has been located. Polygon *K1E'U'K2* is the unrolled surface of one segment of the uncut conoid. Every other segment of the conoid can be found in the same manner.

To locate the intersections with the cylinders in the unrolled interior surface, the distances between the intersection and the uncut conoid must be transferred to the unrolled view. Distance *K43* in the side view is transferred to line *K1E'* to locate point *43* in the unrolled view, and distance *K33* in the side view is transferred to line *K1E'* to locate point *33* in the unrolled view. The same process can be used to plot all lines on the truncated interior surface of the conoid.

To describe the conoid as an unrolled three-dimensional solid, the exterior surface of the conoidal vault must be unrolled. Reference line *RL5* is used as the base line for the unrolling, and the process for unrolling the interior described in relation to reference line *RL4* is repeated with the exterior lines. Once all lines have been plotted, reference line *RL6* is constructed by drawing a line parallel to reference line *RL5* at distance *KH* in the side view. Importantly, the unrolled surface of the conoid exterior is now flat on the picture plane. Because the interior and exterior surfaces are parallel, it is possible to construct the interior surface of the conoid in relation to the exterior surface. However, to do so, each segment of the conoid must be treated as a separate piece and a separate drawing. This means that while the exterior surface can be described as a single sheet, the interior surface

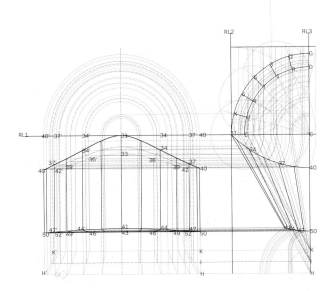

Fig 7.25

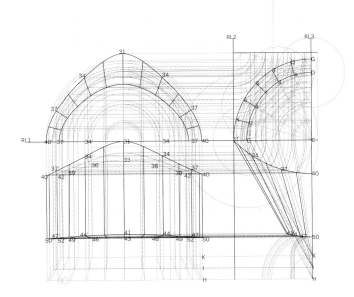

Fig 7.26

must be described as individual segments positioned over the unfolded exterior surface. Therefore, polygon *43,33,35,45*, which describes a segment of the interior surface of the conoidal vault, can be found by plotting it in relation to polygon *41,31,32,42*.

Distance *K1K2* is transferred to reference line *RL6* so that it is centered between the intersection of reference line *RL6* and lines *H1,31* and *H2,32*. These points are labeled *K1'* and *K2'*. Lines are then constructed beginning at *K1'* and *K2'* that are parallel to lines *41,31* and *42,32*, respectively. Distance *K1,43* can be transferred to *K1'43*; distance *K1,33* can be transferred to *K1'33*; distance *K1,45* can be transferred to *K1'45*; and distance *K1,35* can be transferred to *K1'35*. The polygon drawn through the newly located points, *43, 33, 35,* and *45*, describes the interior surface of a segment of the conoid in relation to the exterior surface. Connecting point *33* to *31*, point *35* to *32*, point *43* to *41*, and point *45* to *32* describes one three-dimensional solid that comprises a part of the conoidal vault. Repeating this process for each subdivision describes the vault as a set of unrolled solids.

Each three-dimensional solid can be used to produce templates for every face needed to construct a model from paper or other materials (FIGURE 7.27). Following from the previous example, solid *43,33,35,45,41,31,32,42* can be unrolled as follows. The drawing on the right edge of FIGURE 7.27 shows all pieces of the vault unrolled on a single sheet. Line *31,41* lies on a plane. To move line *33,43* onto the same plane, it must be rotated perpendicular to the plane on which *31,41* lies. Because line *31,41* lies on the picture plane, the path of rotation about *31,41* describes a line in the drawing. These lines must also be perpendicular to line *31,41*. The depth of each three-dimensional solid can be measured in initial quarter arch *31SG*. Therefore, distance *GD* is the depth of every joint in the conoid. Constructing reference line *RL7* parallel to line *31,41* at a perpendicular distance of *GD* provides the depth of the three-dimensional solid. Furthermore, projecting point *43* perpendicularly to line *41,31* until it intersects reference line *RL7* locates point *43p* on the picture plane. Similarly, projecting point *33* until it intersects line reference line *RL7* locates point *33p* on the picture plane. Polygon *41,31,33p43p* describes one face of a three-dimensional segment of the conoid. Unrolled point *33p* must also lie on face *31,33,35,32*. Constructing an arc centered on point *31* through point *33p* until it intersects the projection of point *33* perpendicular to line *31,32* locates point *33pp* on face *31,33,35,32*. Repeating this process for every point on solid *43,33,35,45,41,31,32,42* results in an unrolled drawing with all faces of the solid shown in true proportional dimensions.

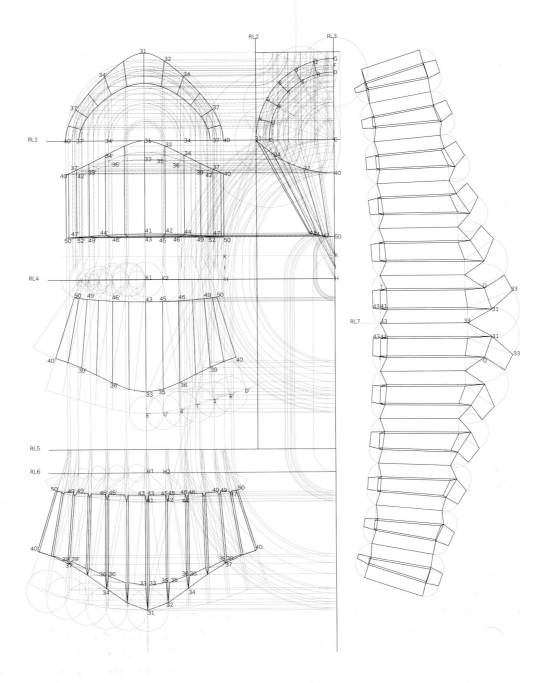

Fig 7.27

Trattato IV, Lastra VIII, Figura 3 Explained

Guarini provided two chapters and ten observations on spherical vaults.[22] The observation explained here is the only one that describes the sphere through solid pieces that can be understood as individual stones.[23] The projection begins with semicircle *ABC* (FIGURE 7.28). The semicircle is divided into two halves: the left half is an elevation, and the right half is both a top view and a section. The right half described by quarter arc *HBC* is divided into five equal segments. Lines are then drawn from points *C*, *5*, *4*, *3*, *2*, and *B* back to the center of the semicircle. Quarter arc *HEF* is constructed outside quarter arc *HBC*. The distance between these two quarter arcs describes the thickness of the dome. Points *5*, *4*, *3*, and *2* are then projected parallel to line *AC* until they intersect line *HB*. Arcs drawn through these intersections and centered on point *H* result in the arcs ending at points *6–9*. These arcs (in dashed lines) are quarters of planar sections taken through semisphere *ABC* at the height defined by points *2–5*. Line *H2* is divided by these arcs, with each division describing the joint between the interior faces of the solid pieces that comprise the dome. Line *H2* is in the top view; to describe it in a front view, points *27, 26, 25, 34*, and *2* are projected parallel to line *BH* until they intersect line *HF*. They are then rotated 180 degrees about point *H* until they intersect line *AH*, thereby translating the horizontal location of points *27, 26, 25, 34*, and *2* from the top view to the elevation. Each point is then projected vertically until it intersects the horizontal projection of points *2–5*. Therefore, point *23* is located at the intersection of the rotation and projection of point *24* with the horizontal projection of point *2*. Points *22, 21*, and *20* can be found in the same manner.

Quarter ellipse *HBG* is the front view of line *H2*. Each elliptical curve in the front view can be found in this manner. The completed drawing describes the three-dimensional properties of a hemispherical dome (FIGURE 7.29).

A sphere is a double-curved surface that cannot be unrolled. Cones are single-curved surface that can be unrolled as has been demonstrated in previous examples. In this example, Guarini used cones to unroll the spherical surface of the dome by finding cones with profile lines parallel to the chords of each of the five subdivisions of the semicircle (FIGURE 7.29). A line is passed from *B* through *2* until it intersects reference line *RL1* at point *Z*. This line is the profile line of the cone with a vertex at *Z* and a base with a radius equal to distance *BH*. The same process can be used to locate the vertices of the cones a points *Y, X*, and *W*. Chord *5C* already intersects reference line *RL1* and, therefore, defines the last and smallest cone.

The outer surface of the sphere must be unrolled with a different set of cones (FIGURE 7.30). A line is passed from point *E* through point *10* until it intersects the reference line at point *Z2*. This line is the profile line of the cone with a vertex at *Z2* and a base with a radius equal to distance *QH*. As mentioned earlier, the right half of the dome is both a top view and a section. The cones have been drawn in section, but in the next step, they are translated to the top view and used to unroll the sphere.

The sphere has been equally divided into five segments. This means that by solving any one of the five segments, the entire sphere is solved. In this

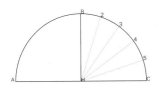
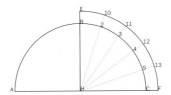
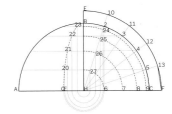

Fig 7.28

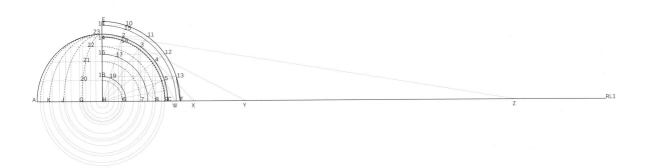

Fig 7.29

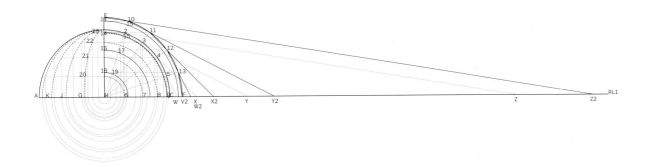

Fig 7.30

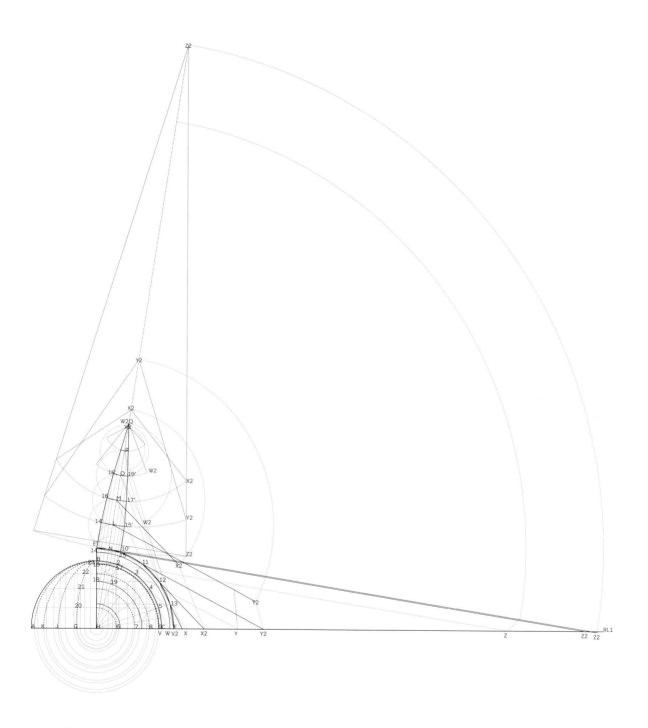

Fig 7.31

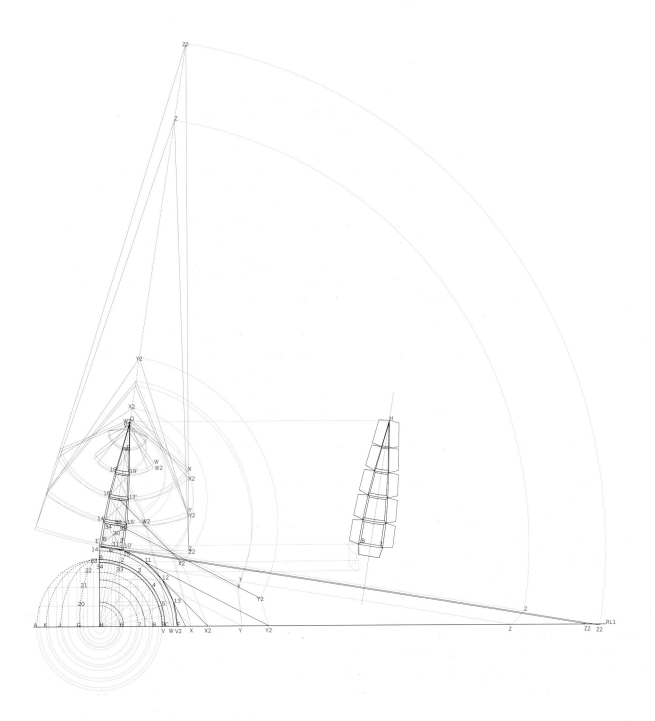

Fig 7.32

example, the segment defined by triangle *E,10,H* is used to unroll the outer surface of the dome. To begin, a centerline is extended from *H* through the midpoint of chord *E10* (FIGURE 7.31). The extension of chord *E10* and its intersection with reference line *RL1* at point *Z2* is transferred to the centerline as an arc rotated about point *N*. Point *Z2* is then labeled, and an arc is drawn that passes through point *N* and is centered on point *Z2*. Points *E* and *10* are then projected parallel to centerline *HZ2* until they intersect the arc established by radius *Z2N* at points *E'* and *10'*. Points *E'* and *10'* have now been located on the unrolled curve of cone *Z2EH*. Distances *E10, 10,11, 11,12, 12,13,* and *13F* are transferred consecutively along centerline *HZ2*, beginning at point *N*. Each of these points, *L, M, O, P,* and *Q*, lies on the joints between the five subdivisions of the triangular piece of the sphere defined by points *H, E,* and *10*. These points are used to transfer the corresponding radius of each unrolled cone to centerline *HZ2*. Therefore, distance *10Y2* is transferred to point *L* as an arc that intersects centerline *HZ2* at point *Y2*. A drawn arc centered at *Y2* and passing through point *L* describes the curve of the unrolled cone on which points *14* and *15* are located. Points *14* and *15* are projected from the quarter arc upward and are parallel to centerline *HZ2* until they intersect the arc that passes through point *L* at points *14'* and *15'*. The shape defined by points *14'*, *15'*, *10'*, and *E'* describes the unrolled exterior face of one of the five solids that comprise triangular division *E,10,H* of quarter sphere *HEF*. Each of the other five pieces can be found in a similar manner and describes the unrolled exterior surface of the sphere defined by the wedge-shaped piece or gore *E'10'Q*.[24]

To unroll the interior face of dome *ABC* in relation to the exterior surface, Guarini struck diagonal lines through each of the five pieces of the unrolled exterior gore (FIGURE 7.32). The intersection of the diagonal lines becomes a reference point for the remainder of the construction. Two lines are constructed within piece *E'10'15'14'*, line *14'10'*, and line *E'15'*. The point of intersection between these two lines is point *30*, the center of polygon *E'10'15'14'*. Chord *B2* defines the linear distance across the interior face of the dome and between points *B* and *2*. Transferring this distance symmetrically about point *30*, on centerline *HZ2*, locates points *31* and *32*. Transferring distance *BZ* as an arc centered on point *31* locates point *Z* on centerline *HZ2*. A drawn arc centered on *Z*, passing through point *31*, defines an arc that is the unrolled curve of the cone on which points *B* and *2* must lie. Projecting points *B* and *2* parallel to centerline *HZ2* locates points *B'* and *2'*. Transferring distance *2Y* as an arc centered at point *32* locates point *Y* on centerline *HZ2*. An arc centered on point *Y*, passing through point *32c*, defines an arc that is the unrolled curve of the cone on which points *33* and *34* must lie. Projecting points *33* and *34* parallel to centerline *HZ2* locates points *33'* and *34'*.

Shape *33'34'B'2'* is the interior face of three-dimensional solid *14'15'E'10'2'33'24'B'*. A similar process can be used to complete the construction of the remaining four pieces of the gore. Because the sphere was equally divided at the start of the projection, repeating this gore for each quadrant of the domes results in a complete dome. The gore is, at this point, a set of solids that have been unrolled from the sphere. To construct them, each solid now must be individually unrolled onto a plane. The projection for this has been pulled to the right of the drawing (FIGURE 7.32). The procedure is identical to the procedure for unrolling the solid piece of the conoid (FIGURE 7.27).

Trattato IV, Lastra XIV, Figura 3 Explained

While Guarini's construction for an ellipsoidal dome uses orthographic projection, its primary operation is based on the proportional relationship between nonparallel lines.[25] The projection begins by defining arch *A5C* on reference line *RL1* (FIGURE 7.33). The points on the exterior curve of the arch are then projected perpendicularly to reference line *RL1* until they intersect reference line *RL2* at points *A'*, *1–9*, and *C*. These points are then projected perpendicularly to line reference line *RL2*. The heights of the arches are then transferred, via orthographic projection, above to reference line *RL2* so that they describe a set of lines above and parallel to reference line *RL2*. The intersection of the lines running parallel to reference line *RL2* and those running perpendicularly to it define a set of points. Therefore, point *4'* is located by the vertical projection of point *4* from reference line *RL2* and the projection of the perpendicular distance of point *4* to reference line *RL1*. Distance *4,5* is stretched by projecting it from reference line *RL1* to reference line *RL2*, creating the new distance, *4'5'*, but the height of *4* and *4'* remain the same. The same operation can be used for the remaining points, and curve *A'5'C* can be constructed through them. The semicircle that defines the outer curve of arch *A5C* is stretched along one axis, thereby converting it to a semiellipse. The amount of distortion is contingent upon angle *CA'A* relative to reference line *RL1*. If the angle is zero degrees, curve *A'5'C* is a semicircle. As the angle approaches ninety degrees, the length of curve *A'5'C* increases. The operation therefore proportionally stretches the semicircle into a semiellipse.

Semiellipse *A'5'C* now defines the outer surface of an ellipsoidal dome. The following construction focuses exclusively on the dome's outer surface to simplify the explanation of the drawing (FIGURE 7.34). Guarini explained that a perpendicular section through the dome defined by curve *A'5'C* can be taken by transferring the lengths of the centerlines on semiellipse *A'5'C* from point *Q* to center at point *X* and before rotating them until they intersect the corresponding height. Therefore, distance *Q1'* is transferred with parallel lines to point *X* and then rotated until it intersects a line constructed parallel to reference line *RL1* from point *1* at point *1"*. The remaining points can be achieved in the same manner. The curve drawn through these points is semiellipse *L5M*.

At this stage, Guarini reminded the reader that parallel sections through an ellipsoid are similar and, therefore, proportional variations of one another. This is an important distinction because the operation he used to calculate the sections is not a modern orthographic projection but rather an exercise in calculating proportional figures. The initial illustration of this process simplified the construction to its basic geometric framework (FIGURE 7.35). In the second proposition of book six, Euclid stated, "If a straight line be drawn parallel to one of the sides of a triangle, it will cut the sides of the triangle proportionally."[26] Guarini used this principle to calculate the distance from the center of the ellipsoid to points on a set of parallel sections. The beginning of the construction is the striking of a line from A to A' to create reference line $RL4$. This line defines right triangle CAA'. Furthermore, line $A'A$ is parallel to line QX. Based on Euclid's proposition, it is clear that the proportional relationship between line segments $A'Q$ and QC is the same as the proportional relationship between line segments $A'X$ and XC. In addition, any line drawn from C that ends at line $A'A$ preserves this proportional relationship between the segments created by its intersection with line QX. Guarini capitalized on this relationship by first doubling and then transferring the distance of the lines that originate at point Q and terminate at $1'-5'$ to point C. He doubled the lines to convert them from the variable radii of the semiellipse to variable diameters. This is because $A'C$ is a diameter, and to calculate proportional variations of it, diameters must also be used. Therefore, radius $Q1'$ is transferred to reference line $RL1$ and is doubled. Its intersection with reference line $RL4$ creates point $1D$. Line $C1D$ is equal to twice the length of $1'Q$. Completing this operation for points $1'-5'$ locates all diameters of the ellipse of which semiellipse $A'5'C$ is a part within right triangle $AA'C$.

The next portion of the construction entails dividing the lines constructed in the previous step proportionally to find the radii of the elliptical sections on centerlines of ellipse $A'5'C$ (FIGURE 7.36). This information provides the points through which each elliptical section passes. The projection of point $1'$ onto reference line $RL2$ is point 1. The line constructed from point 1 perpendicularly to reference line $RL1$ is parallel to line AA'. It therefore cuts lines $C1D$–$C5D$ proportionally, creating segments $C10$–$C14$. These segments are the diameters of an ellipse; when they are cut by line QX, they become radii. Transferring

these radii to the corresponding centerline in semiellipse $A'5'C$ results in the plotting of an elliptical section through the ellipsoidal dome. Therefore, distance $R10$ is transferred to $Q10$; distance $N11$ is transferred to $Q11$; distance $P12$ is transferred to $Q12$; distance $S13$ is transferred to $Q13$; and distance $T14$ is transferred to $Q14$. Because a semiellipse is bilaterally symmetrical, these distances can be mirrored across line $Q5'$, and all points on the new ellipse can be located. Following the same procedure, the projections of points $2'-5'$ locate the remaining four sections through the ellipsoidal dome (FIGURE 7.37).

The final portion of the construction is the unrolling of each triangular piece, or gore that subdivides the dome. In this example, the gore defined by triangle $4'6'Q$ is used (FIGURE 7.38). To begin, Guarini returned to section $L5M$ and extracted the dimensions along the curve to unroll each piece of the dome. This works because at the outset Guarini set the base for the dome as a circle. Distance $5W$ describes the linear distance between points Q' and 45 on unrolled gore $4'6'Q$. Therefore, transferring distance $5W$ to point $5'$ along the extension of centerline $Q5'$ locates point 45. Points 44 and 46 are then projected parallel to centerline $Q5'$ until they intersect the projection of point 45 parallel to chord $45,46$. The triangle is the first piece of unrolled gore $4'6'Q$. The remainder of the pieces can be found in the same manner (FIGURE 7.39).

The interior surface of the unrolled gore can be found by giving the vault thickness with a second ellipse (dashed line) and then repeating the same procedure as above (FIGURE 7.40). Unlike the hemispherical dome, the ellipsoidal dome is not identical through rotation, so the procedure must be repeated

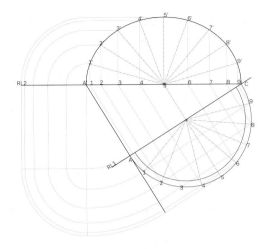

Fig 7.33

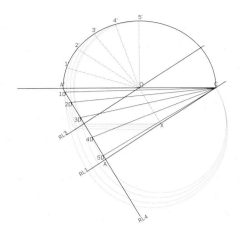

Fig 7.35

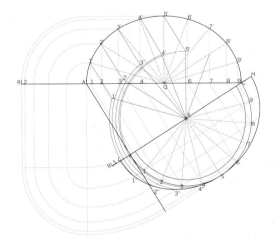

Fig 7.34

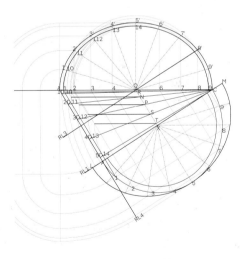

Fig 7.36

for the remaining pieces of the dome. Each quadrant of the dome is identical, so once all pieces of a quadrant have been solved, the dome is complete.[27] Furthermore, because Guarini set the dome on top of a circular section, the dome could be unrolled using cones as in Guarini's spherical dome. The cones have been added to FIGURE 7.41 without additional explanation, as the procedure is nearly identical to that described in "Trattato IV, Lastra VIII, Figura 3 Explained."

Trattato IV, Lastra XIV, Figura 8 Explained

The last chapter of "Dell'ortografia gettata" (i.e., chapter eight) has only one observation: the development of a toroidal vault.[28] The projection begins with semicircle ABC (FIGURE 7.42). The points on the semicircle are projected parallel to line BB' until they intersect line AC. Arcs are drawn centered at point V and passing through each point of intersection. The arcs are terminated at ninety degrees and a vertical line (parallel to line BB') is constructed. Perpendicular to this line, line VF, an arc of the same diameter as arc ABC, is constructed. A second arc is constructed on the same center with a smaller radius to provide the vault's thickness. Arc segment AF is the outer edge of the top view of toroidal vault ACDF. Arc AF is equally divided into eight pieces that are, in turn, divided to locate centerlines on each piece. The divisions are then connected back to point V. This defines toroidal vault ACDF with a plan radius equal to line VA, an internal sectional radius equal to line KH, and an external sectional radius equal to line KE.

The points on the interior section of the vault, arc GHI, are projected parallel to line EK until they intersect line DF (FIGURE 7.43). These points of intersection are rotated 180 degrees about point V. Line GV is constructed from the terminus of the arc back to center point V. Arc GHI and its centerlines are reconstructed perpendicular to line GHI. This operation has rotated the interior surface of toroidal vault ACDF out from under the exterior surface so that it can be treated as a separate projection that maintains its relationship with the overall vault through a connection to a common center: point V.

Once the geometry of the vault has been clearly established and separated into interior and exterior surfaces, it can be unrolled upon a plane (FIGURE 7.44). A torus is a double-curved surface that cannot be unrolled, so it must be approximated with another surface that can be unrolled. To accomplish this, Guarini employed cones. Each chord of semicircle ABC is extended until it intersects the extension of line GV. Chord AQ is extended until it intersects the extension of line GV at point Z. Point Z is the vertex of a cone with axis ZV and a circular base of radius AV. The process is repeated for each chord on semicircle ABC. A total of eight cones are identified.

The same process is repeated for the interior surface of the vault described by arc GHI, identifying an additional eight cones on the horizontal extension of line AV (FIGURE 7.45). To describe the surfaces that connect the interior and exterior surfaces of toroidal vault ABCD, cones are identified that are coincidental with the joint lines. Therefore, joint line PP' is extended until it intersects the horizontal extension of line AV at point R. This process is repeated for all remaining joint lines. Once the centers of the cones' vertices have been located, arcs are constructed through the endpoint of

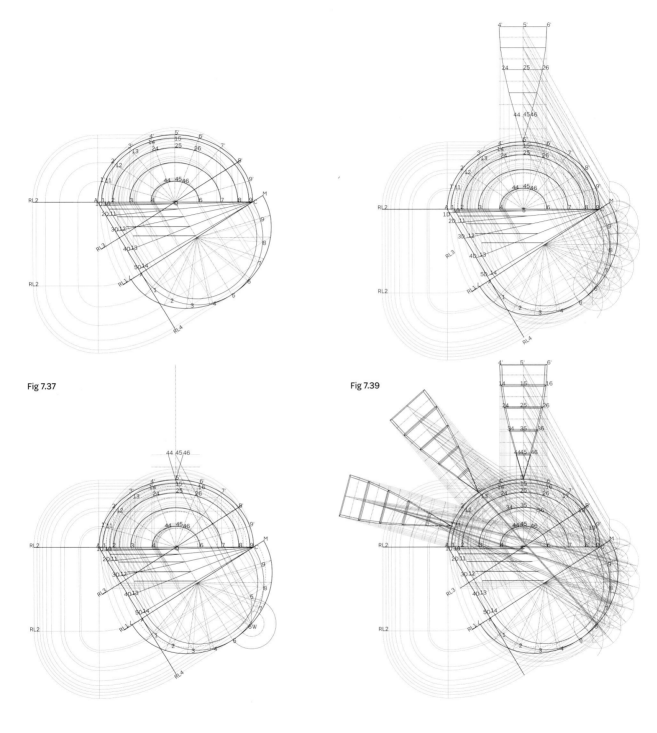

Fig 7.37

Fig 7.38

Fig 7.39

Fig 7.40

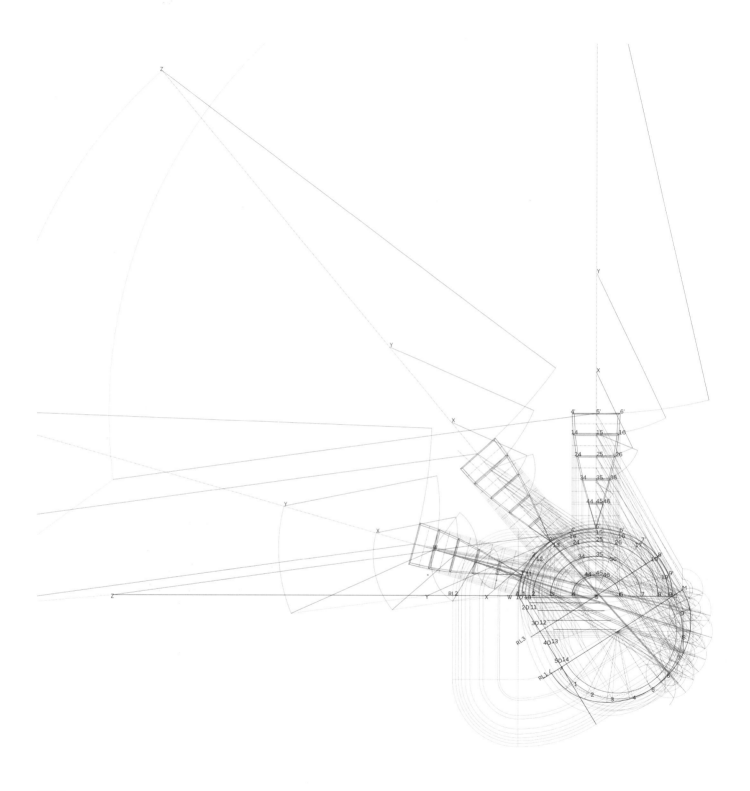

Fig 7.41

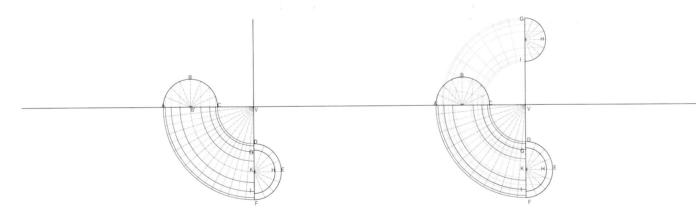

Fig 7.42   Fig 7.43

each chord. These arcs describe the unrolled surface of the cones on which the unrolled toroidal vault is located. Therefore, radii *ZQ* and *ZA* define a patch of unrolled conic surface on which the toroidal surface defined by points *A*, *Q*, *Q'*, and *F* is unrolled. Radii *S12* and *S13* describe a similar patch of unrolled surface on the interior of the vault, and radii *RP'* and *RP* define a patch of conic surface between the exterior and interior surface of toroidal vault *ACDF*.

For a conic surface to be unrolled, lines must be ruled upon it, running from its vertex to equally divided segments along its circular base. In this case, the divisions are equal to the eight divisions of arc *AF* constructed at the outset of this example. This translates the ruling lines of the cones into joint lines on the unrolled surface of the toroidal vault (FIGURE 7.46). Therefore, distance *A1* is transferred from arc *AF* to the arc defined by radius *ZA* to locate point *1'*. Distance

A1' is transferred eight times along the arc defined by radius *ZA*. The points are then connected back to point *Z* to describe the joints on the unrolled outer surface of the toroidal vault. Similarly, the arc defined by radius *ZQ* can be divided by transferring distance *9,2* to *Q2'* and then transferring this eight times across the arc. The point can be connected back to point *Z* to define the ruling lines on the unrolled surface. The remaining six pieces of the exterior surface of toroidal vault *ACDF* can be found in a similar manner.

The same process as above can be repeated for both the interior surface of the vault and the surfaces of the joints. Once all conic surfaces have been unrolled upon a plane, the projection is complete, and all information necessary to construct a model of the toroidal vault from paper or another material is present (FIGURE 7.47).

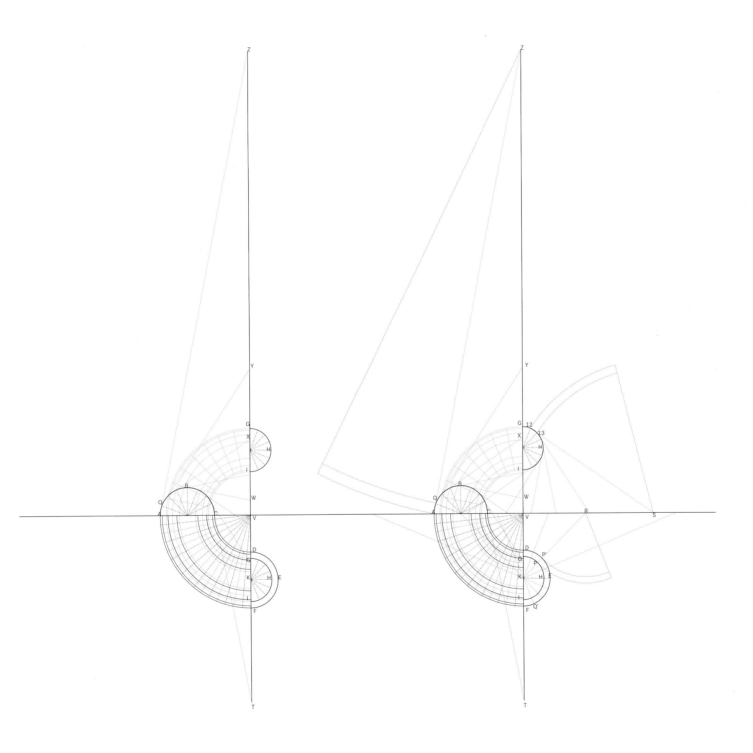

Fig 7.44

Fig 7.45

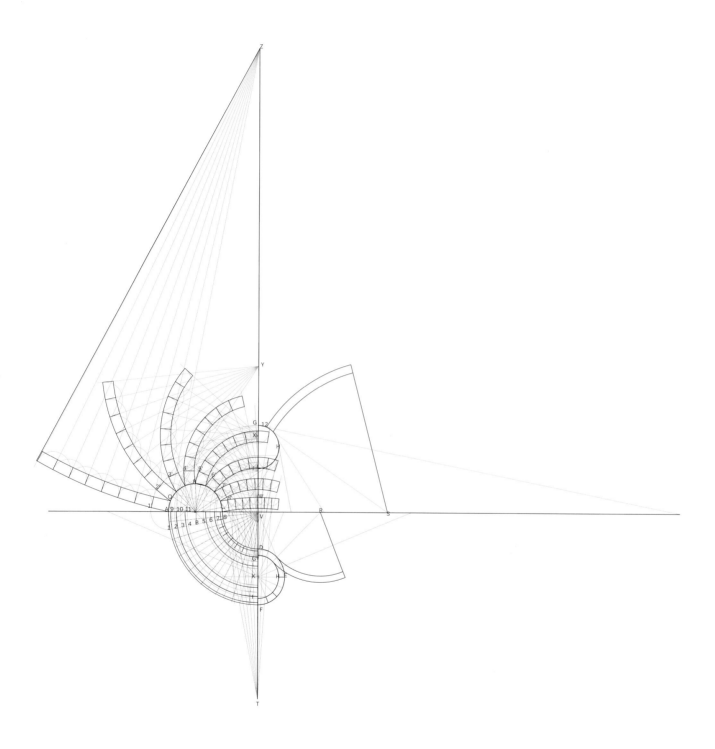

Fig 7.46

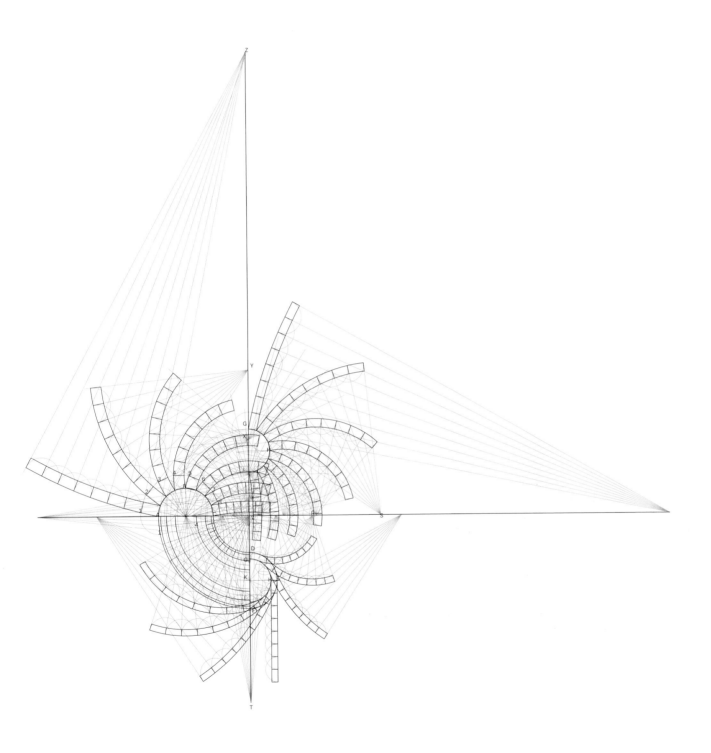

Fig 7.47

1   Guarini, *Architettura civile*, 192.

2   See, e.g., "Osservazione decima" in ibid., 242.

3   Euclid, *Thirteen Books*, 100.

4   See "Osservazione nona" in chapter three of the fourth tractate in Guarini, *Architettura civile*, 206–7.

5   See "Osservazione decimaquarta" in chapter three of the fourth tractate in ibid., 217–20.

6   See Girard Desargues, "The Rough Draft on Conics," in Field and Gray, *Geometrical Work of Girard Desargues*, 100–1.

7   The projection is constructed so that the semicircle is centered on the axis of the cone. Moving point *V* to the left or right in the top view results in an asymmetrical projection.

8   Hilbert and Cohn-Vossen, *Geometry and the Imagination*, 7–11.

9   See "Osservazione unica" in chapter eight of the fourth tractate in Guarini, *Architettura civile*, 264–5.

10 Ibid., 198–201.

11 This conic plot method is covered in "Osservazione decima" in chapter three of the fourth tractate in ibid., 208–9.

12 An example of this method is given in "Osservazione duodecima" in chapter three of the fourth tractate in ibid., 211–14.

13 This could also be unrolled from the side projection, but for consistency, the unrolling is explained in the same manner as for the other projections.

14 See Guarini, *Architettura civile*, Trattato IV, Lastra III.

15 See ibid., 208–10.

16 Müller asserted a second error by Guarini here. However, in this case, Müller measured the drawing and found it to be different than the instructions in the text and incorrect. The reconstruction deployed here follows the text and not the drawing. See Müller, "Authenticity of Guarini's Stereotomy," 205.

17 Guarini, *Architettura civile*, 225–7.

18 All the following steps depend on the operation described in figure 7.2.

19 The angle of rotation has no consequence on the calculations of the drawing. It is more of a question of layout and legibility.

20 Guarini, *Architettura civile*, 230–4.

21 Ibid., 234.

22 Ibid., 245–59.

23 Ibid., 255–7.

24 This method, as described by Guarini, is like the method for projecting a sphere into a set of triangular patches called gores. The difference here is that Guarini used polycentric cones in lieu of cylinders. For a discussion of the different methods for unrolling a sphere, see Joseph Gwilt, *The Encylopedia of Architecture* (London: Longmans, 1867), 326.

25 Guarini, *Architettura civile*, 260–2.

26 Euclid, *Thirteen Books*, 100.

27 Guarini's projection for each gore is different than what is described here. Guarini transferred the distances from the original drawing with circles along a centerline and connected each point of intersection with an approximated curve. The projection in this text transfers the distance with projection lines and connects the points of intersection with straight line segments. This was done to connect the development to the dome section via orthographic projection. For Guarini's specific method, see Guarini, *Architettura civile*, 262.

28 Ibid., 264–5.

Acknowledgments

The work for this book began in 2012. Since that time, no other group has supported my research more than the students of the Woodbury University School of Architecture. They have worked diligently in seminars and studios to explore issues related to descriptive geometry, stereotomy, and drawing in general. While no student work appears in this book, students' contributions through enthusiasm and the production of rigorous drawings has been essential.

My colleagues at Woodbury University have been an important network. I am grateful for their contributions. Dr. Ewan Branda provided insightful critique of the work at all stages of development. Duane MacLemore has been a frequent collaborator in teaching and our discussions on geometry have been central to the development of this book. Anali Gharakhani, once a student, and now a colleague has seen and commented on the work over a period of six years. Ingalill Wahlroos-Ritter supported my teaching and research as chair and continues to do so as dean. Louis Molina mentored me as a teacher and offered on-demand help with the Italian language. Marc Neveu proposed the idea of a book in 2014, and helped to guide me through the process of obtaining a publisher. Joshua Stein's comments on the text helped to clarify the role of drawing conventions in relationship to Guarini's work. I would also like to thank Lisa Little at USC for her careful reading of an early draft.

In the time that I have been a faculty member at Woodbury, two important colleagues passed away. Nick Roberts supported the work as chair, arguing for the importance of geometry in the curriculum. He was warm and caring mentor, and his presence is missed daily on campus. Dean Norman Millar supported me as a young faculty member through impromptu phone calls of encouragement and sharp critique. He was a wonderful dean and person, and he is missed.

As a teacher, I am grateful for the important professors that I have encountered in the course of my education. Several key instructors at SCI_Arc helped to encourage my interests in drawing and geometry. Jay Vanos introduced me to descriptive geometry. Russell Thomsen provided endless encouragement and inspiration. Oliver Touraine, Doris Sung, Mitchell Dejarnett, and Gary Paige all played important roles in introducing me to architectural drawing. Perry Kulper was and continues to be an important figure in my development. He challenged me as a student and continues to do so. I am grateful for his instruction, and for the writing that graciously contributed to this book. The Department of Art History at Rutgers University introduced me to formal analysis and to the value of historical inquiry. Dr. Jane Sharp and Dr. Carla Yanni were inspiring faculty, who had significant impact on my education.

Jeremy Quinn and Michelle Jaquis allowed me to work in their studio in China Town during my sabbatical in 2018. Their work and our discussions provided the rich atmosphere in which much of the content of "Guarini Animated" was developed.

Cameron Macdonell's copyediting far exceeded reasonable expectations. He helped to restructure the text, correct translations, and question key arguments. I learned a lot about writing, simply by reading his comments.

Jessica Greenfield transformed a collection of drawings into a book. She brought an understanding of 18th-century publication that helped to build subtle formal connections with *Architettura civile*.

Applied Research and Design of Oro Editions made this book possible. Gordon Goff created a clear route for making this publication a reality. Jake Anderson's organization and technical knowledge were indispensable.

I am grateful to the publications and conferences that included early versions of the work contained in this book: *Log*, *306090*, the Museum of Modern Art, *JSAH*, *JAE*, ACADIA, and ACSA.

Financial support was provided by the Woodbury University School of Architecture through Dean Ingalill Wahlroos-Ritter. Additional support was provided by the Woodbury University Faculty Association.

My family have been be my biggest supporters. I am forever grateful to my parents: Elaine, Joe, Mark, and Robin. I would be nowhere without my bothers: Bret, Peter, and Joseph. Monroe and Camille have been patiently sharing their father with this book. Katherine Harvey encouraged me when the book seemed to be an impossibility. She found solutions to problems that I found intractable. This book would not be here without her contributions.

Image Credits:

All images and drawings were produced by Mark Ericson unless otherwise noted.

Ordinary Geometry
1.1 Guarini, *Architettura civile* (Turin: G. Mairesse, 1737), Trattato IV, Lastra XIV.

On Redrawing
2.1 Guarini, *Architettura civile*, Trattato IV, Lastra XI, Figura 4
2.2 Ibid., Trattato IV, Lastra IX
2.3 Ibid., Trattato IV, Lastra IV

Reassembling Guarini
3.1 Guarini, *Architettura civile*, Trattato IV, Lastra iX
3.5 Ibid., Trattato IV, Lastra XIV, Figura 3
3.7 Albrecht Dürer, Underweysung Der Messung
    (Nürnberg: Formschneider, 1538).
3.8 Juan Caramuel Lobkowitz, *Architectura Civile Recta y Obliqua*
    (Vigevano: Camillo Corrado, 1678). Parte 2, Lamina 9.
3.17 Guarini, *Architettura civile*, Trattato IV, Lastra IV, Figure 1–3
3.19 Ibid., Trattato IV, Lastra XIV, Figure 8
3.21 Ibid., Trattato IV, Lastra IV, Figure 4, 5
3.23 Ibid., Trattato IV, Lastra XIII, Figura 1

Animating Guarini
5.1 Guarino Guarini, *Architettura civile*, Trattato IV, Lastra IV, Figure 4, 5
5.3 Francesco Borromini, plan of San Carlo alle Quattro Fontane, Rome, 1634
    (Albertina Museum, Vienna, Graphische Sammlung, Az. Rom. 171).
5.4 Guarino Guarini, *Architettura civile*, np.
5.9 Ibid., Trattato IV, Lastra VII, Figura 4